This JMJ Journal Belongs To:

_____

As I search for words in this journal, may I also seek God's wisdom in my heart.

A Journey of Light, Faith, and Gratitude

Welcome to the JMJ Journal, a space designed to help you grow closer to God through Scripture, reflection, prayer, and creativity.

Jesus, Mary, Joseph (JMJ) is the holy family that reminds us of faith, love, and trust in God's plan.

This journal is more than a gratitude journal — it's a faith-filled journey of the heart.

Each chapter invites you to slow down, listen to God's voice, and respond with honesty, hope, and joy.

What You'll Discover in Each Chapter

A Short Devotion
Scripture-based thoughts to center your heart on God's truth.

Faith-Inspired Activity Page
Enjoy a custom word search and maze that reinforce the day's theme

Reflection + Journaling Page
Answer simple prompts to connect with God and grow in gratitude

Dear Lord, About Today...
A lined space to write prayers, thanks, or thoughts to God

Coloring Page
Relax and reflect on Scripture through art and color.

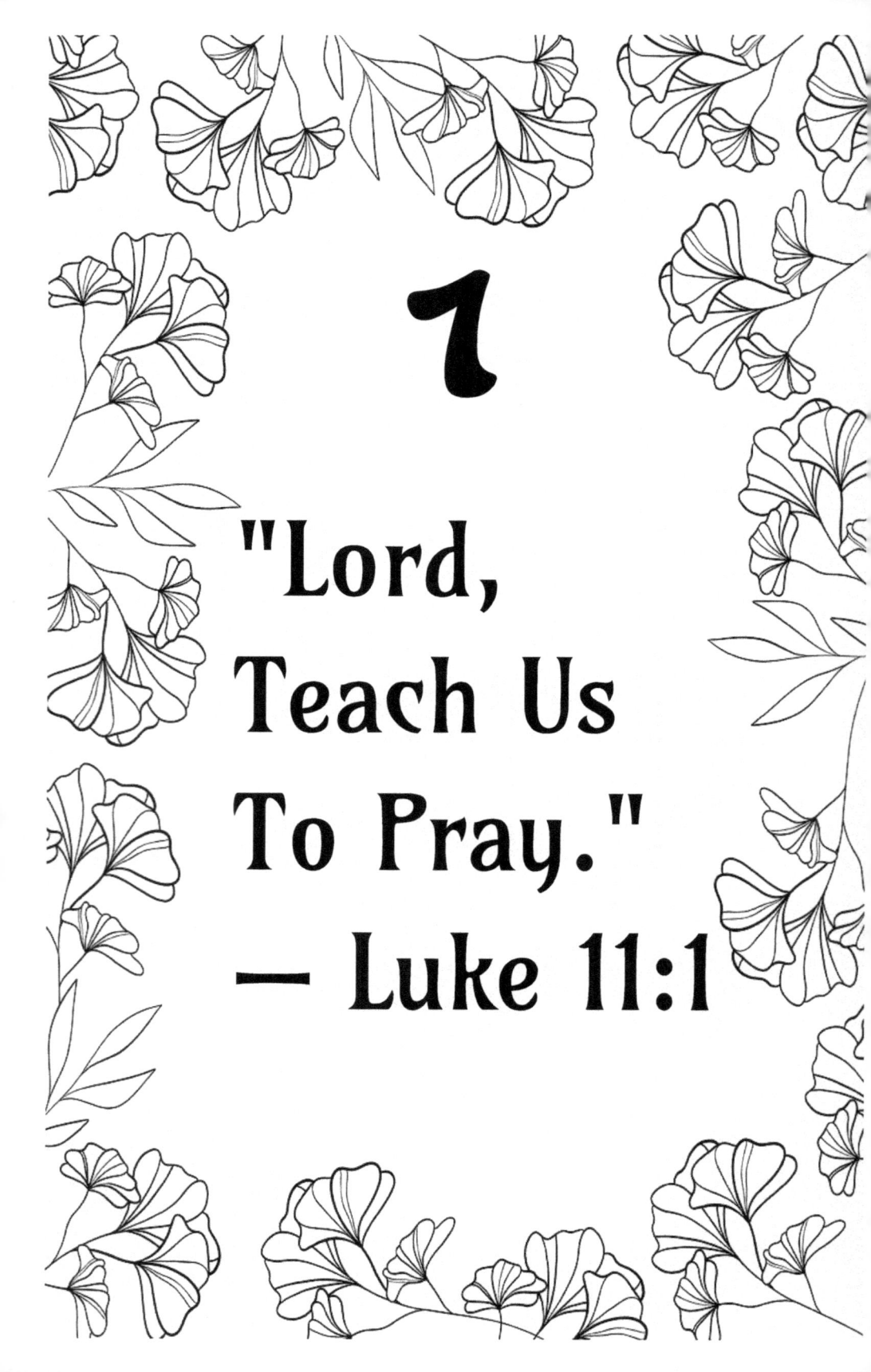

1

"Lord,
Teach Us
To Pray."
— Luke 11:1

When God Speaks

Jesus' disciples asked Him how to pray, He gave them the perfect example—the Lord's Prayer. This prayer is more than a set of words; it is a guiding principle for how we communicate with God. It teaches us to honor God, seek His will, ask for our needs, and receive forgiveness. It also reminds us that God is our loving Father, always near, always listening. Each phrase of this prayer encourages us to develop a deeper relationship with God, trusting Him in both times of need and times of thanksgiving.

✝ Prayer is a foundation of faith, a moment where we pause and reconnect with God. Whether we are young or old, just beginning our faith journey or strengthening it, the Lord's Prayer provides guidance, peace, and encouragement in every season of life.

The Lord's Prayer

Our Father who art in heaven,
hallowed be thy name.
Thy kingdom come.
Thy will be done
on earth as it is in heaven.
Give us this day our daily bread,
and forgive us our trespasses,
as we forgive those who trespass against us,
and lead us not into temptation,
but deliver us from evil.

For thine is the kingdom and the power, and the glory,
forever and ever.

Amen.– Matthew 6:9

The Lord's Prayer

```
            F  Y  L  U  R  A
            Y  A  E  M  A  N
            S  U  T  V  Q  P
            U  Q  D  H  R  F
            S  R  E  E  E  D
            E  X  W  Q  M  R
         V  J  O  O  M  T  W  E
R  H  E  A  V  E  N  P  L  L  O  D  T  O  V  B  W  M  T  J
T  D  T  G  R  D  S  T  G  L  Z  A  S  C  R  I  N  Y  R  C
U  I  W  O  T  E  M  P  T  A  T  I  O  N  L  S  L  H  R  G
A  S  F  J  B  E  W  I  P  H  S  L  B  L  T  Q  H  E  O  L
L  J  P  Z  P  I  U  V  O  Z  U  Y  X  F  B  K  Y  I  D  X
E  K  M  O  D  G  N  I  K  O  R  B  O  S  T  B  E  D  P  R
            Q  P  G  F  T  R  I  U
            R  L  Q  G  E  O
            A  Y  I  X  A  S
            Y  V  R  V  D  N
            E  C  W  O  E  L
            R  F  R  M  L  M
            L  V  A  C  O  G
```

PRAYER	NAME	DEBTS	POWER
JESUS	KINGDOM	TEMPTATION	FOREVER
FATHER	WILL	DELIVER	AMEN
HEAVEN	DAILY BREAD	EVIL	TRUST
HALLOWED	FORGIVE	GLORY	WORSHIP

Reflection

"PRAYER IS THE RAISING OF ONE'S MIND AND HEART TO GOD." – ST. JOHN DAMASCENE

TODAY I WILL FOLLOW GOD'S LIGHT BY...

....

....

CHOOSE A SMALL ACTION, ATTITUDE, OR WORD TO CARRY WITH YOU!

Name one way you've seen God present in your life this week:

....

....

....

Which line of the Lord's Prayer speaks to you the most? Why?

....

....

....

....

Jesus, give [_____] peace today. Teach them—and me—to love like You.

....

NAME TWO AMAZING THINGS THAT HAPPENED TODAY:

☐ ....

....

☐ ....

....

Today, I am Grateful for...

....

....

....

Dear Lord
About Today...

"Pour out your heart before Him; God is a refuge for us." –
Psalm 62:8

Our Father's Maze Adventure

Start here

"Lead me, Lord, in
Your path of truth."
— Psalm 25:5

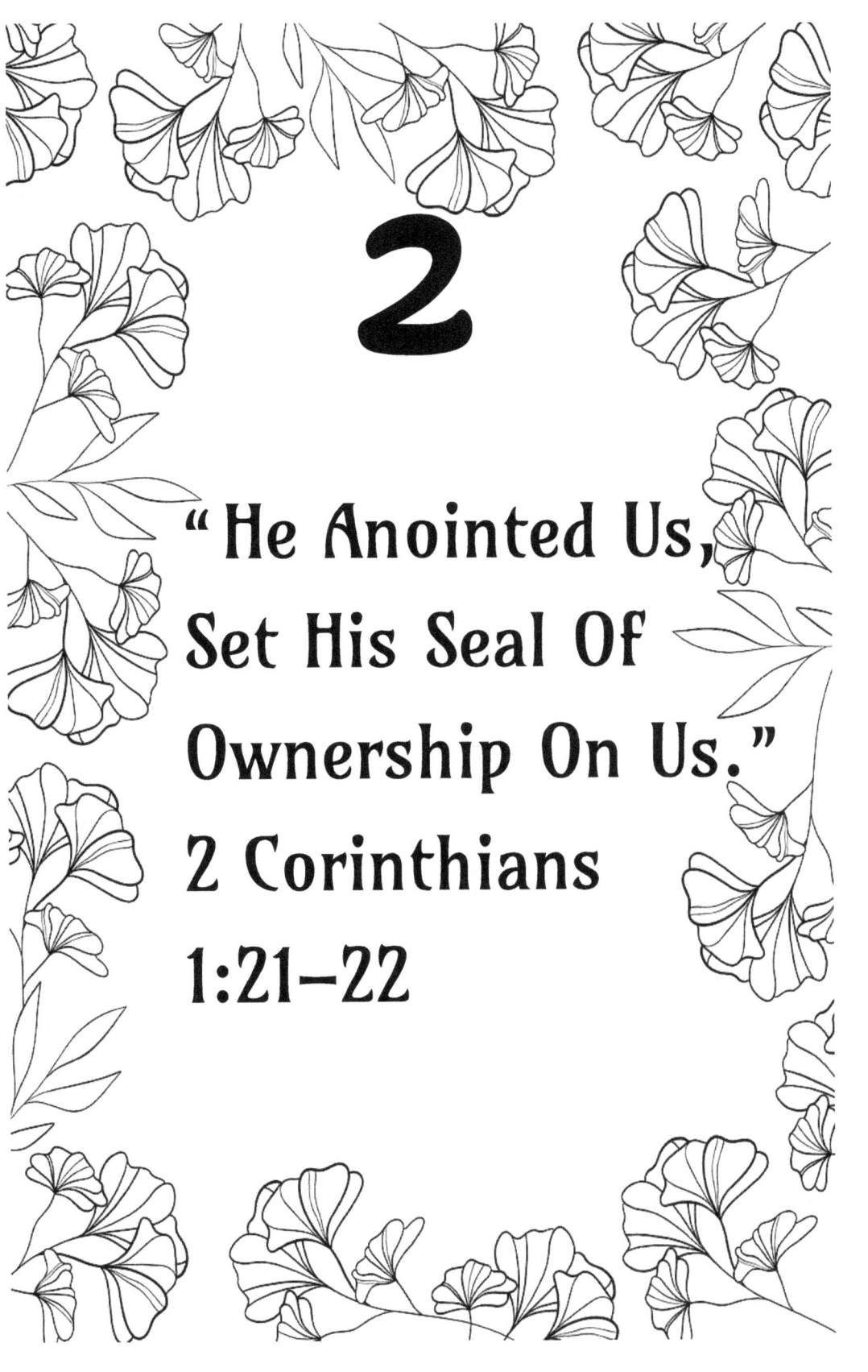

2

"He Anointed Us, Set His Seal Of Ownership On Us."
2 Corinthians 1:21-22

The Holy Spirit & Peace

When Jesus was baptized, a dove appeared, representing the presence of God's Spirit.

In Noah's story, a dove carrying an olive branch signaled the end of the flood.

Today, the dove reminds us of God's peace and guidance in our lives. The Holy Spirit is not just a symbol but a living presence — bringing comfort in times of fear, clarity in moments of confusion, and calm in the middle of life's storms.

Come Holy Spirit

```
E  T  B  W  D                          Y  R  O  L  G
   A  R     E  B                     I  K     R  J
I     B  I  W  C  F                V  F  U  A  Y     W
H  L  L  Y  N  P  A  Z           P  R  A  I  S  E  K  U
   E  E  L  K  I  I  R  A        X  V  T  Q  L  D  U
      S  P  E  U  T  E  G     L  E  Y  Y  C  Q  S
   O  S  G  U  P  H  Y        L  I  A  T  J  S  W
      I  P  D  B  S  C  K     C  P  R  U  E  R  O
      N  B  I  N  Q  O  N     F  I  Z  S  G  Y  R
      G  C  H  R  Y  R  G     M  C  U  G  V  R  C
         O  V  I  Q              S  J  N  W
         P  L  L  T  S           M  I  A  E  H
         E  M  W  A  S           E  D  T  V  L
         F  L  A  W              R  F  J  A
         V  W  X                 Z  E  E
      M  A  Y  Z  G  E        T  B  Q  H  Y  M
   R  F  T  X  I  Z  C           O  V  L  U  A  P  P
L  M  I  N  E  M  A  Z  E     Z  W  O  R  S  H  I  P  F
C  O  P  Q  D  E  B  S        H  A  I  S  S  E  M  K
N  V  M  K  P  R  N  Z        S  M  O  D  K  F  L  R
```

FAITH	PRAISE	PEACE	GLORY
GRACE	HEAVEN	HOPE	DISCIPLE
JESUS	SALVATION	MESSIAH	WORSHIP
HOLY	BLESSING	SPIRIT	AMEN
GOSPEL	MIRACLE	TRINITY	CROSS

Reflection

"THE FRUIT OF THE SPIRIT IS LOVE, JOY, PEACE, PATIENCE, KINDNESS, GOODNESS, FAITHFULNESS." – GALATIANS 5:22

TODAY I WILL FOLLOW GOD'S LIGHT BY...

....

....

CHOOSE A SMALL ACTION, ATTITUDE, OR WORD TO CARRY WITH YOU!

How have you experienced the peace of God this week?

....

....

....

How has God's peace helped you through a difficult time?

....

....

....

....

Lord, fill [_____] with Your peace today. Please bring them comfort & strength.

....

NAME TWO TIMES WHEN YOU EXPERIENCED UNEXPECTED PEACE OR CALM:

☐ ....

....

☐ ....

....

Today, I am Grateful for...

....

....

....

Dear Lord
About Today...

"For those who are led by the Spirit of God are children of God." – Romans 8:14

Led by the Spirit

"Since we live by the Spirit,
let us keep in step with the
Spirit."
— Galatians 5:25

Start here

3

"Even The Wind And The Sea Obey Him."

– Mark 4:41

Jesus Calms the Storm

While crossing the Sea of Galilee, a fierce storm struck. Waves crashed, and the disciples panicked, fearing for their lives. Jesus, asleep in the boat, awoke to their cries. He stood and commanded, "Peace, be still." Instantly, the storm calmed.

✝ Life can feel overwhelming, like a raging storm. But Jesus is always with us, bringing peace even in the chaos. When fear takes over, trust in Him—He is in control.

Peace, Be Still

```
          Q  F  U
          T  M  S
          Y  L  U
          N  M  A  S
          J  C  I  X  C  E
          V  O  R  A  R  D  J
       F  Q  E  A  M  O  Q  T  K
    E  E  Y  C  C  M  I  N  S  W
 R  I  A  Z  Z  L  I  V  Y  U  T  H
I  D  R  R  V  C  E  G  A  O  R  J  O  Y
O  P  H  X  P  S  O  D  S  K  T  W  P  R
G  P  B  L  T  A  O  B  E  U  Q  D  I  E  R  M

Z  L  O  B  E  Y  E  E  C  A  E  P  W  A  V  E  S  G  D  L
W  P  M  Q  N  M  S  S  S  V  G  C  P  S  B  L  H  H  F  G
D  A  S  E  L  P  I  C  S  I  D  O  D  I  N  T  Z  A  H  J
F  V  T  J  E  O  A  R  H  U  W  D  K  E  L  S  I  B
    E  A  R  S  T  R  E  N  G  T  H  U  T  Q
    R  E  U  T  R  I  I  H  Y  U  H
    P  A  W  P  Y  K  J
```

STORM	WAVES	BOAT	POWER
FAITH	WIND	MIRACLE	HOPE
JESUS	FEAR	WATER	GOD
PEACE	CALM	OBEY	SAVIOR
DISCIPLES	TRUST	PRAYER	STRENGTH

Reflection

"DO NOT BE AFRAID,
FOR I AM WITH YOU."
— ISAIAH 41:10

CHOOSE A SMALL ACTION,
ATTITUDE, OR WORD TO
CARRY WITH YOU!

What is something in your life right now that feels like a storm?

....
....
....
....

What is one thing you can do when you start to feel worried or afraid?

....
....
....
....

Lord, please bring peace to [_____] as they carry their cross with faith and strength.

....

NAME TWO TIMES TODAY
WHEN YOU FELT CALM,
EVEN IN A STRESSFUL
MOMENT.

☐ ....
....

☐ ....
....

Today, I am
Grateful for...

....
....
....

Dear Lord
About Today...

"He got up, rebuked the wind and said to the waves,
'Quiet! Be still!'"-Mark 4:39

 Peace, Be Still

Start here

"Cast all your anxiety on him because he cares for you."
—1 Peter 5:7

4

"Be Kind And Compassionate To One Another."

Ephesians 4:32

Love Thy Neighbor

One day, a lawyer asked Jesus, "Who is my neighbor?" In response, Jesus told the story of The Good Samaritan: A man was attacked by robbers and left on the road. A priest and a Levite walked by without helping, but a Samaritan—a man from a group despised by Jews—stopped, cared for his wounds, and took him to safety. Jesus asked, "Which of these was a neighbor?" The answer was clear: The one who showed mercy!

✝ Loving our neighbor means showing kindness to everyone, not just those who are easy to love. Whether it's a friend, a stranger, or even someone difficult, Jesus calls us to act with compassion and mercy.

 # Love in Action

```
                    R  E
                 E  F  M  R
              G  T  E  O  Z  O
           N  H  R  O  D  R  P  B
        A  E  C  A  R  R  Y  G  N  H
     R  U  Y  U  M  Y  G  O  V  I  E  G
  T  C  O  M  P  A  S  S  I  O  N  V  V  I
S  S  I  R     A  M  J  G        H  E  R  E
A  E  E  N  G     X  G  C  O        P  T  J  E  N
R  P  K  A  C  T  I  O  N  D  N  E  I  R  F  E  N  S
   C  T  C  K  K  N  H  K  I  R  H  Z  A  L
   X  I  N  I  Y  T  I  S  O  R  E  N  E  G
   O  R  J  N  K  N  T  G  W  D  X  E  G  P
   H  A  E  D  D        O  B  W  A  C
   E  M  J  N  X     B  X     N  E  A  D  E
   A  A  J  E  C     L  N     K  V  C  N  R
   R  S  O  S  V     I        E  O  S  A  A
   T  D  I  S  S     O  F     Y  L  X  B  C
```

FORGIVE	NEIGHBOR	CARE	DONKEY
KIND	LOVE	RESCUE	OIL
ACTION	KINDNESS	STRANGER	BANDAGE
FRIEND	MERCY	HEART	GENEROSITY
SERVE	SAMARITAN	CARRY	COMPASSION

Reflection

"LET US NOT LOVE WITH WORDS OR SPEECH BUT WITH ACTIONS AND IN TRUTH." – 1 JOHN 3:18

TODAY I WILL FOLLOW GOD'S LIGHT BY...

....
....

CHOOSE A SMALL ACTION, ATTITUDE, OR WORD TO CARRY WITH YOU!

What is one small way you can show love to someone today?

....
....
....

Name one way someone has shown kindness to you recently. How did it make you feel?

....
....
....

Lord, help me see [_____] the way You do—with love and kindness.

....

NAME TWO TIMES WHEN YOU CHOSE KINDNESS OR PATIENCE, EVEN WHEN IT WAS HARD.

☐ ....
....

☐ ....
....

Today, I am Grateful for...

....
....
....

Dear Lord,
About Today...

"Love your neighbor as yourself." - Luke 10:27

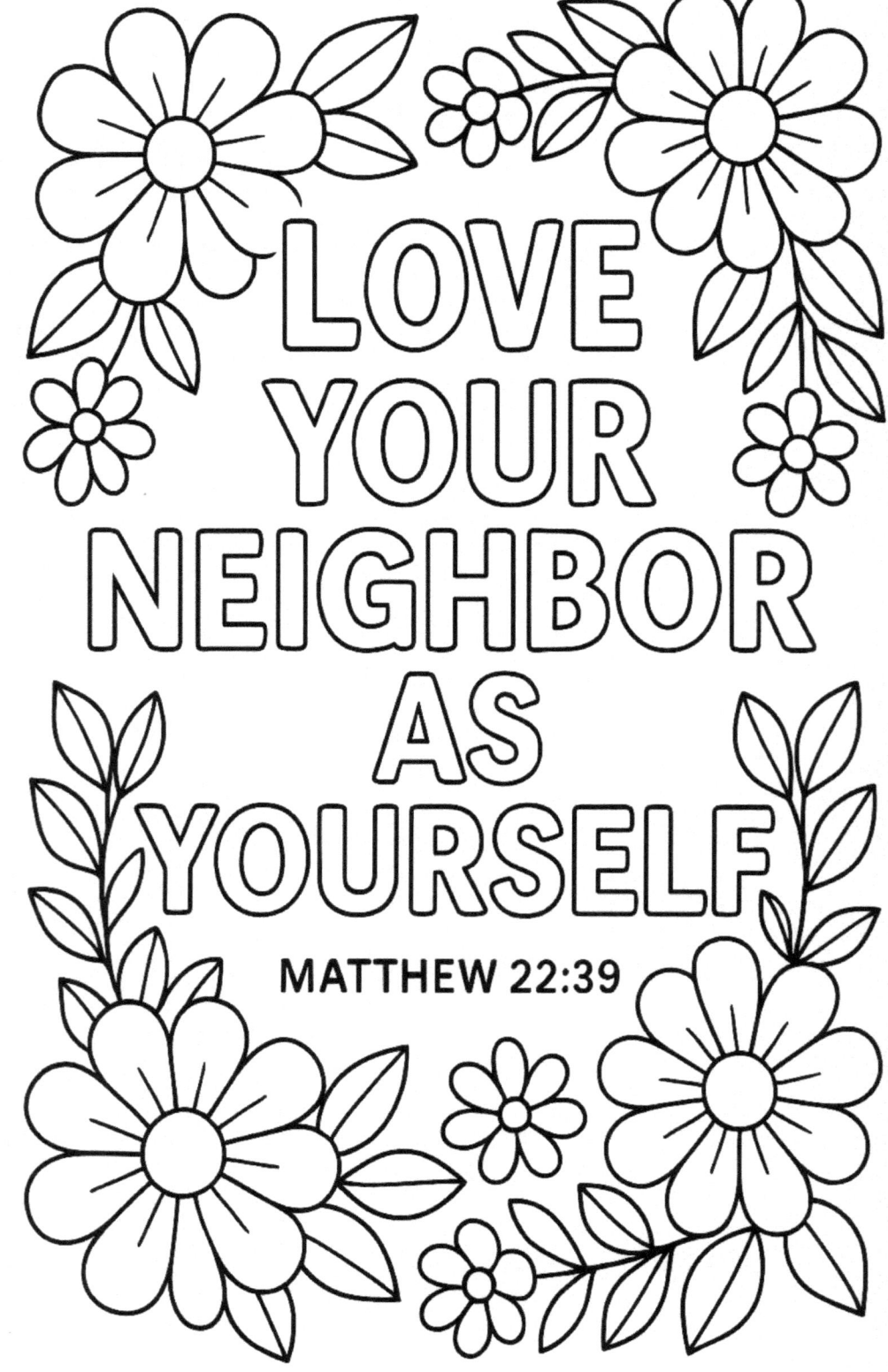

A Good Neighbor

 Start here

"Do to others as you would have them do to you."
— Luke 6:31

5

"The Lord Is My Light And My Salvation."
– Psalm 27:1

Eyes of Faith

One day, Jesus met a man who had been blind since birth. People wondered why the man couldn't see, but Jesus told them, "This happened so God's power could be seen." Then, Jesus gently made mud, placed it on the man's eyes, and told him, "Go wash in the pool." The man did what Jesus said—and suddenly, he could see for the very first time! Everyone was amazed! The man was filled with joy and told others what Jesus had done.

† Sometimes we can't see what God is doing, but faith helps us trust Him anyway. Jesus still opens eyes..not just physical, but spiritual so we can see His truth and goodness.

Now I See

```
R  W  L  I  G  H  T  M        W  R  Z  T  O  U  C  H
F  A  J  D  N  S  M  A        A  O  G  C  S  N  Y  T
E  Y  H  T  U  R  T  M        B  A  N  H  A  U  C  T
Z  I  S  O     M  I  X        S  D  T     C  R  H  F
K  L  R  P     R  V  O  I  C  E  I  R     G  E  T  B
U  E  Y  E  M  A  B  A  T  L  R  A  M  L  K  D  V  M  Q  F
I  B  E  K  C  H  L  C     K  F  E  R  O  T  S  E  R  P
S  G  L  S  G  I  H  S        I  V  Y  Y  A  K  G  O
H  E  A  L  I  N  G           T  I  E  N  M  O  C
W  U  F  M  D                 K  W  S  L  V
```

BLIND	*SEE*	*MIRACLE*	*RESTORE*
HEALING	*WASH*	*BELIEF*	*VOICE*
MUD	*POOL*	*TRUST*	*TOUCH*
EYES	*SILOAM*	*LIGHT*	*MERCY*
FAITH	*ROAD*	*TRUTH*	*HOPE*

Reflection

"OPEN MY EYES THAT I MAY SEE WONDERFUL THINGS IN YOUR LAW." – PSALM 119:18

TODAY I WILL FOLLOW GOD'S LIGHT BY...

....

....

CHOOSE A SMALL ACTION, ATTITUDE, OR WORD TO CARRY WITH YOU!

How did you respond when something didn't go your way?

....

....

....

Name one area in your life where you're asking God for clarity or direction.

....

....

....

Lord, bring light to [_____] Show me how to care for them.

....

....

NAME TWO TIMES TODAY WHEN YOU BROUGHT LIGHT OR HOPE TO SOMEONE, LIKE JESUS DID FOR THE BLIND MAN

☐ ....

....

☐ ....

....

Today, I am Grateful for...

....

....

....

Dear Lord
About Today...

"I was blind but now I see!" -John 9:25

From Blind to Blessed

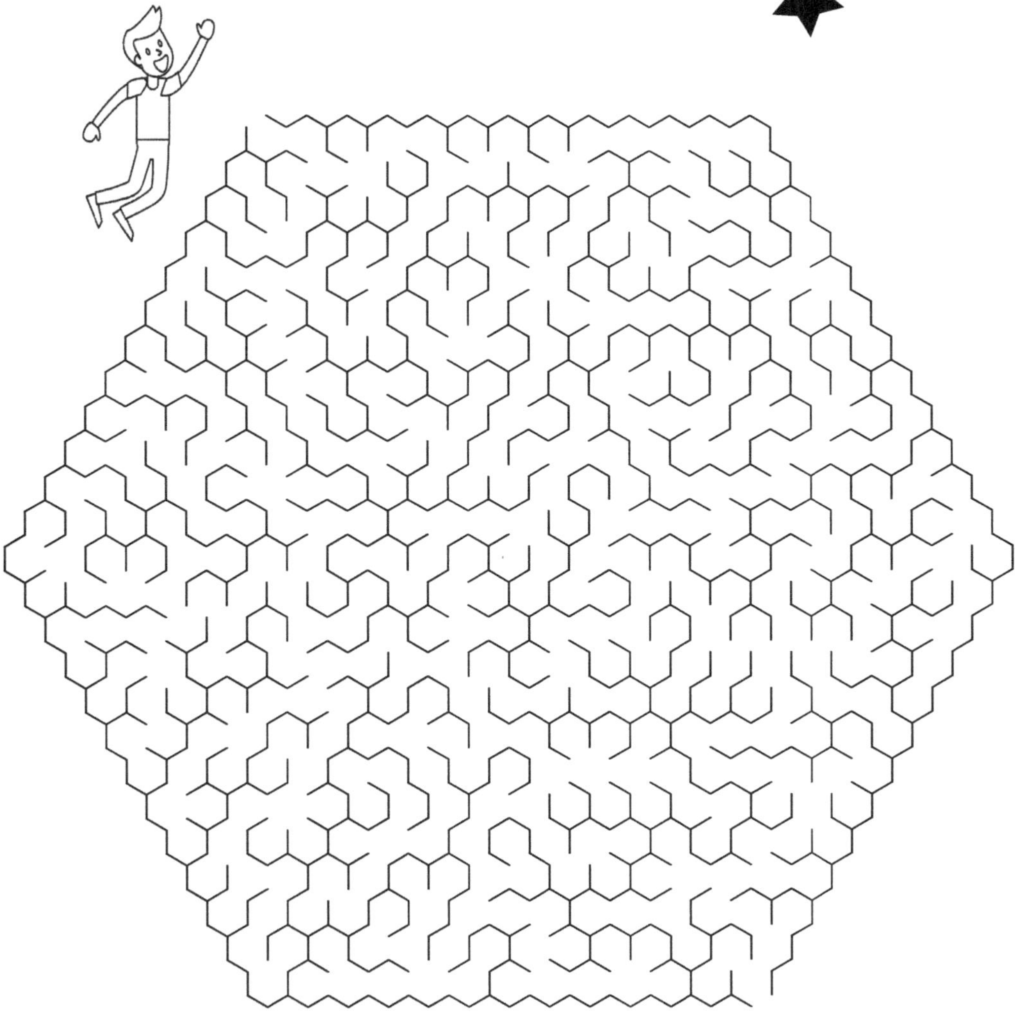

"Jesus said, 'Receive your sight; your faith has healed you.'"
— Luke 18:42

Start here

6

"Arise, Shine, For Your Light Has Come."
–Isaiah 60:1

Guided by the Light

Three wise men followed a bright star in the sky, searching for the newborn King. The star led them to Bethlehem, where they found Jesus with Mary. They worshiped Him and offered gifts of gold, frankincense, and myrrh. Their hearts were filled with joy, for they had found the Savior. Then they returned home a different way, listening to God's warning in a dream.

✝ God still leads us and sometimes not with stars, but with peace, truth, and His Word. When we follow His light, we find the path to joy, purpose, and hope.

Guided By The Light

```
W           C           A           M           X
    O           S           S           W           G
Y       L           T           T       G           I
  R       L       A       A       A           F       Z
    A       O K K J R B E N Z M T       P
O       M   F F V U V L B G E S T   I
  Y       Y B E T H L E H E M R M H           A
    W     P E Z Q P D G S L X G S F   P
        I E S N E C N I K N A R F J R
          S F M R D L O G X O G T O
          L E Z Y U F E V W U N M Y
          B M N R O B W E N I U
          T E A R J P W S K
            N F H V E

          P E A C E
        E P O H N O W
        L I G H T

          U P I
```

STAR
LIGHT
WISE MEN
BETHLEHEM
KING

GIFTS
GOLD
FRANKINCENSE
MYRRH
JOURNEY

WORSHIP
MARY
STABLE
NEWBORN
PEACE

JOY
ANGEL
PROMISE
FOLLOW
HOPE

Reflection

"YOUR WORD IS A LAMP FOR MY FEET, A LIGHT ON MY PATH." – PSALM 119:105

Name one way God has guided you recently, even in a small decision.

....
....
....

Where do you need God's light in your life right now?

....
....
....
....
....

Lord, shine Your light on [_____]. Show me how to support them with Your love.

....

NAME TWO WAYS YOU CAN WORSHIP JESUS IN YOUR EVERYDAY LIFE.

☐......................

....

☐......................

....

Today, I am Grateful for...

....
....
....

Dear Lord
About Today...

"We saw his star when it rose and have come to worship him."--Matthew 2:2

Follow the Star

"I am the light of the world."
--John 8:12

Start here

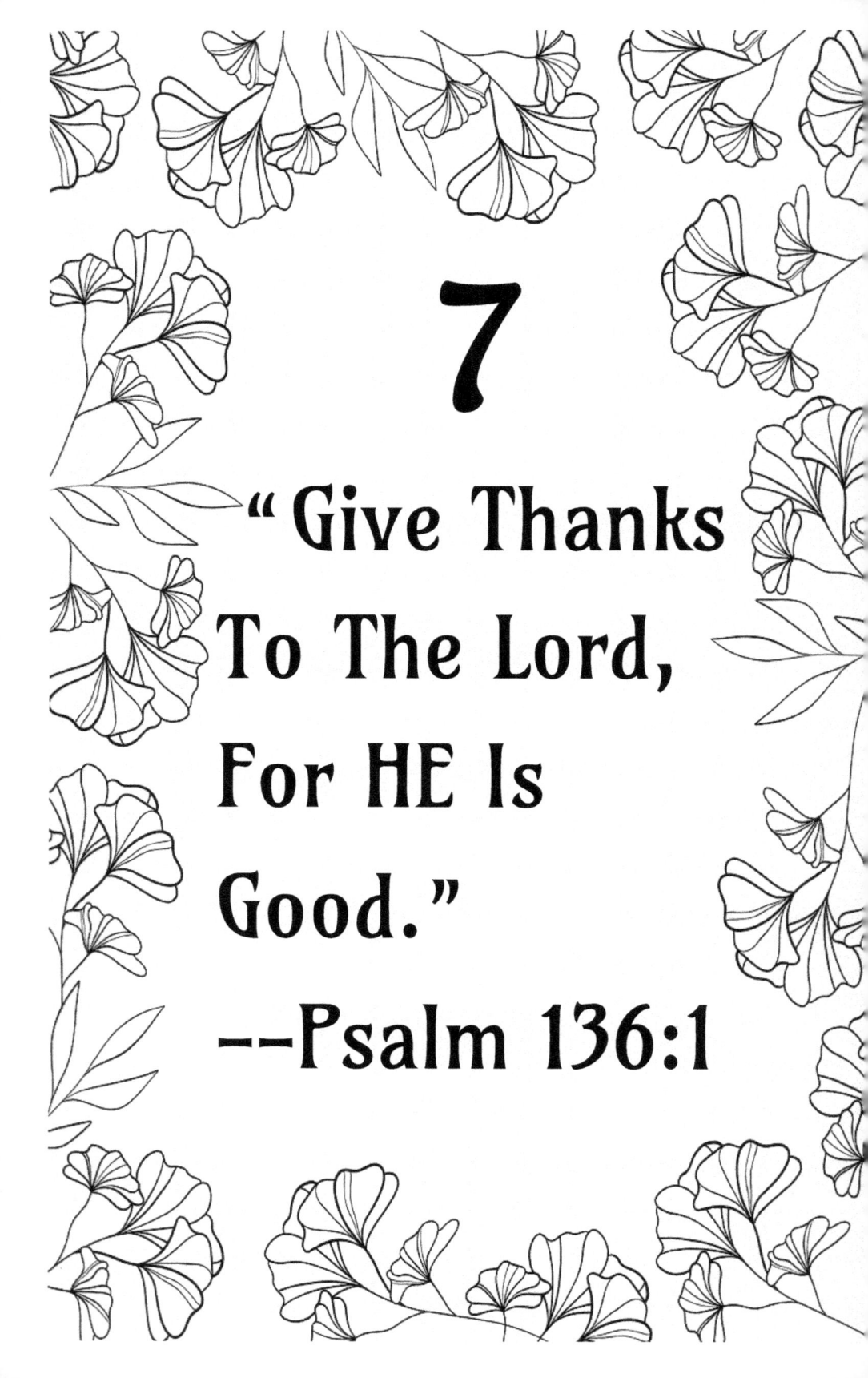

7

"Give Thanks
To The Lord,
For HE Is
Good."
--Psalm 136:1

The Power of Gratitude

Ten men with leprosy called out to Jesus, asking for mercy. Jesus told them to go show themselves to the priests—and as they went, they were healed. But only one man came back to thank Jesus. He was a Samaritan. Jesus praised him, saying his faith and gratitude made him whole.

✝ It's easy to forget to say "thank you," even when God answers our prayers. But gratitude draws us closer to Him. A thankful heart reminds us that every blessing is a gift from a loving God.

A Grateful Heart

```
W  X  S  F  U                             V  R  T  B
H  C  E  M  F  I                       F  L  F  S  C
H  E  T  K  E  N  I                 A  S  O  Q  R  H
Q  U  L  A  M  R  J  U           I  G  E  R  I  E  O
K  J  M  C  N  L  C  O  N     T  O  E  S  S  D  P  I
R  E  C  D  A  E  I  Y  L  Q     H  Q  P  R  A  I  S  E  I
G  S  O  A  E  R  H  N  V  B     C  B  O  O  M  A  O  L  J
O  U  Q  B  L  L  I  U  G  P  L  H  B  G  Y  A  D  K  Z  B
H  S  B  E  C  W  O  M  N  Y  O  E  R  C  M  R  X  J  G  X
I  L  U  F  K  N  A  H  T  M  Y  X  S  M  S  I  T  M  I  O
Y  A  Q  W  D  X  S  M  W  E  E  S  J  S  E  T  F  N  K  V
P  F  O  R  G  I  V  E  N  C  D  O  V  O  I  A  N  U  M  Q
   E  U  O  J  N  X  Y  H  U  U  P  O  P  Z  N  L  V  G  P
      N  T  N  R  U  T  E  R  T  D  I  B  T  E  G  N  R
         J  R  L  U  Z  N  S  I  Y  C  S  W  W  I  T
            O  A  V  E  Z  C  T  M  E  H  Z  L  G
               Y  Y  S  E  S  A  I  C  X  A  C
                  B  J  W  R  V  O  E
                     P  P  G  V  H
                        I  Q  V
```

LEPERS	THANKFUL	PRAISE	RETURN
GRATITUDE	SAMARITAN	CLEAN	OBEY
FAITH	PRIEST	BLESSING	FORGIVEN
MERCY	JESUS	MIRACLE	JOURNEY
HEALING	WHOLE	VOICE	JOY

Reflection

"GIVE THANKS TO THE LORD, FOR HE IS GOOD; HIS LOVE ENDURES FOREVER." – PSALM 107:1

TODAY I WILL FOLLOW GOD'S LIGHT BY...

....

....

CHOOSE A SMALL ACTION, ATTITUDE, OR WORD TO CARRY WITH YOU!

Name one small blessing that made a big difference this week.

....

....

....

What part of your life feels like a gift from God?

....

....

....

....

Lord, shine Your light on [_____]. Show me how to support them with Your love.

....

NAME TWO WAYS YOU CAN WORSHIP JESUS IN YOUR EVERYDAY LIFE.

☐ ....

....

☐ ....

....

Today, I am Grateful for...

....

....

....

Dear Lord
About Today...

"Thanks, God!"

Start here

"I will give thanks to you, Lord, with all my heart." — Psalm 9:1

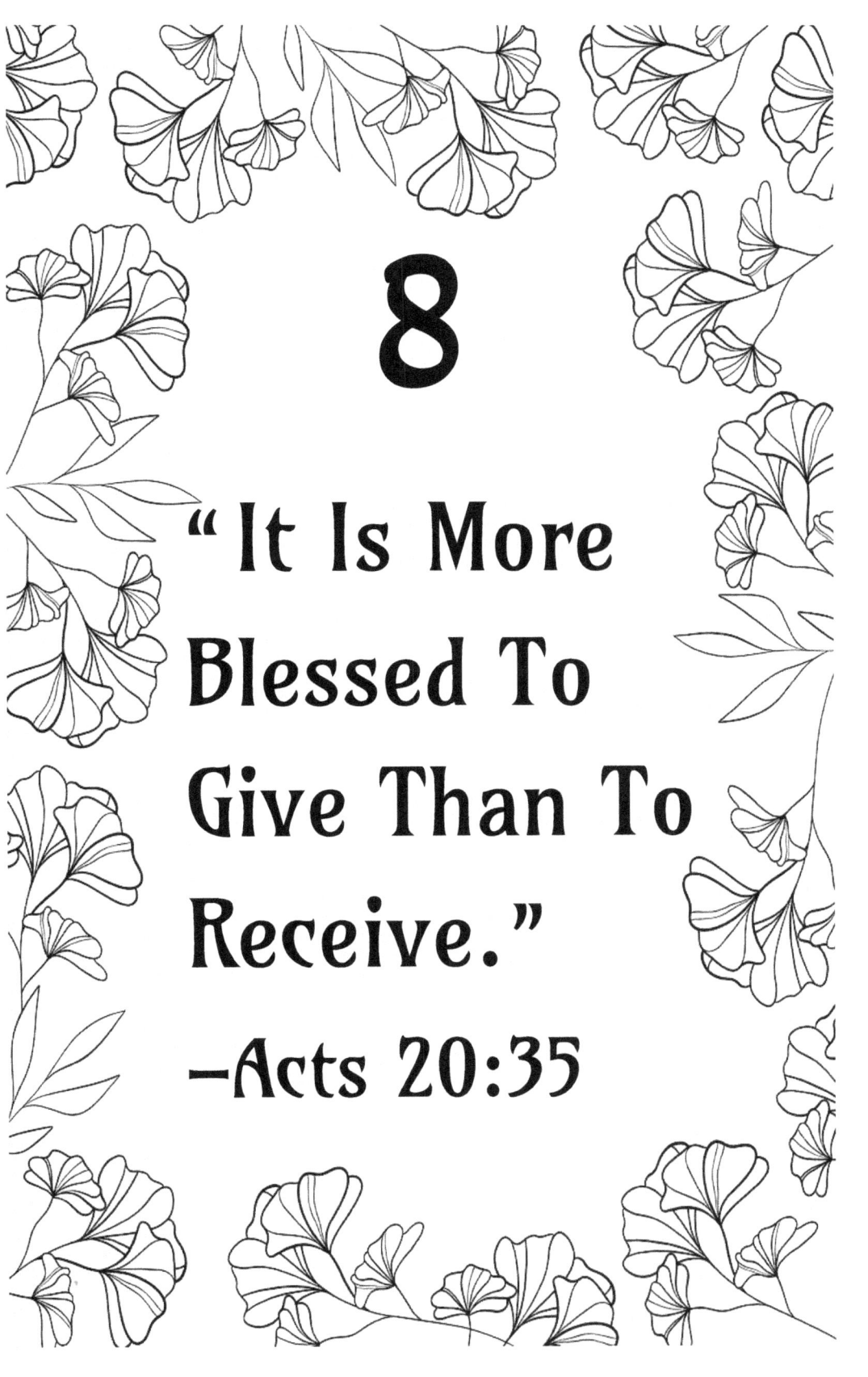

8

"It Is More
Blessed To
Give Than To
Receive."
–Acts 20:35

Giving From the Heart

As Jesus watched people placing offerings into the temple treasury, many rich people gave large amounts. Then, a poor widow came and placed in two small coins. Jesus told His disciples that she had given more than anyone else—because she gave all she had with a trusting heart.

✝God doesn't measure what we give by how much. it's about how we give. Whether it's our time, kindness, or money, giving with love and faith matters more than the size of the gift.

The Widow's Gift

```
        Q  H  H  K  T  Q  U  W  Q  U  H
     V  E  U  W  V  P  C  E  B  G  T  P  J
  N  G  A  I  O  U  S  D  V  Y  Q  N  O  Q  E  W
  H  R  R  D        K  I        R  I  F  E  C  U  W
  T  G  I  F        G  S        N  R  I  P  O  O  R  O
  P  W  O  L        W  C        F  E  Y     P  X  E  T
  C  I  O  R        U  I        Y  F  A
  E  K  H  W        M  P        K  F  F
  L  T  B  S        X  L        J  O  V
     S  U  O  R  E  N  E  G  L  F  H  E
     Q  X  H  O  U  S  O  U  D  T  B  Q
     K  K  C  W  K  N  Q  U  I  E  T  M
           I  T        S  A        M  G  J
  I        O  R        G  F        M  P  G  D
S  J       V  U        I  Y        N  H  L  L
Q  T  E    N  S        F  V        J  L  O  E
N  Q  I  S C  T        T  E        A  V  H  W
X  G  V  M  U  L  I  I  X  H        F  V     E  P  X  A
R  T  R  E  A  S  U  R  E  A  S  N  I  O  C  P  J  P  T
C  J  B  P  V  U  E  Q  M  F        S  C  C  H  F  F  O
```

WIDOW	TEMPLE	TREASURE	DISCIPLES
OFFERING	COINS	JESUS	GIFT
HEART	RICH	POOR	QUIET
GIVE	TRUST	ALL	GENEROUS
FAITH	LOVE	WORSHIP	TRUE

Reflection

"EACH ONE MUST GIVE AS HE HAS DECIDED IN HIS HEART..." –
2 CORINTHIANS 9:7

TODAY I WILL FOLLOW GOD'S LIGHT BY...

....
....

CHOOSE A SMALL ACTION, ATTITUDE, OR WORD TO CARRY WITH YOU!

Name one way you can give with love this week—big or small.

....
....
....

Why do you think Jesus praised the widow's gift more than the others?

....
....
....
....

Lord, help me give like the widow. Show me how to bless
[＿＿＿＿＿] with love and trust.

....

NAME TWO WAYS YOU CAN BE GENEROUS WITHOUT USING MONEY..

☐ ....

....

☐ ....

....

Today, I am Grateful for...

....
....
....

Dear Lord, About Today...

"She, out of her poverty, put in everything—
all she had to live on."--Mark 12:44

"The Widow's Gift"

Start here

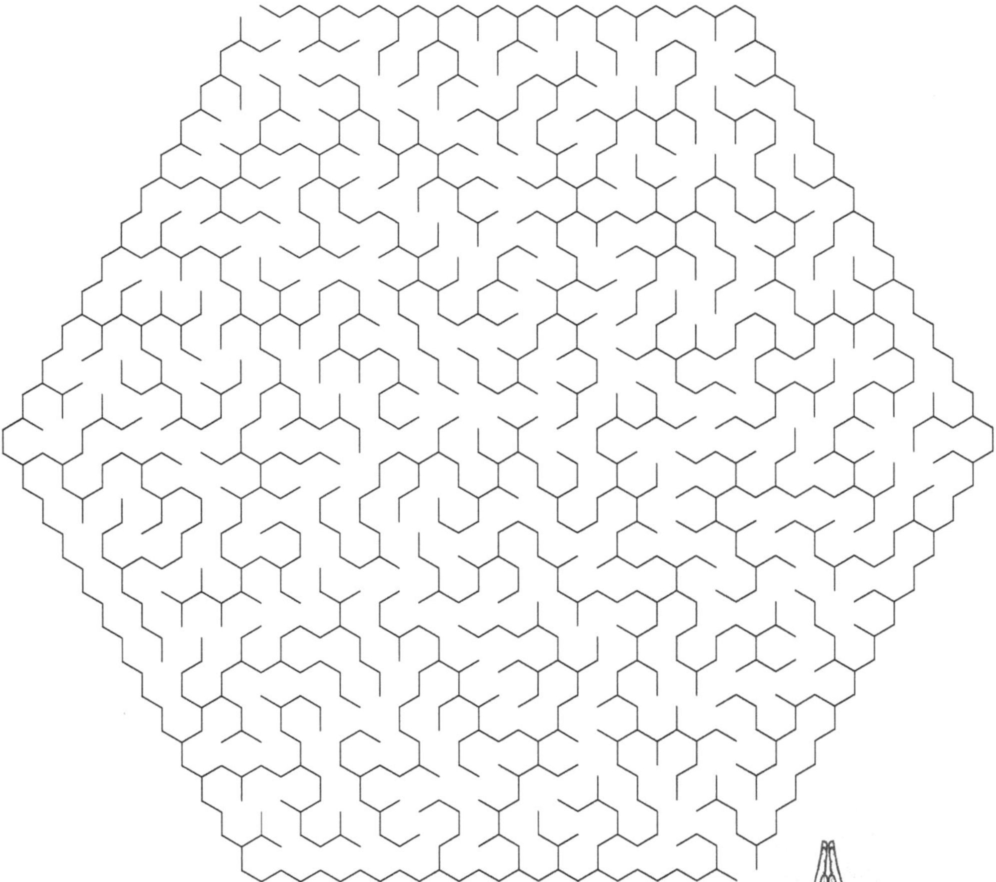

God Loves a Cheerful Giver Verse Coloring Page

God loves a cheerful giver.

2 Corinthians 9:7 HCSB

Blessed

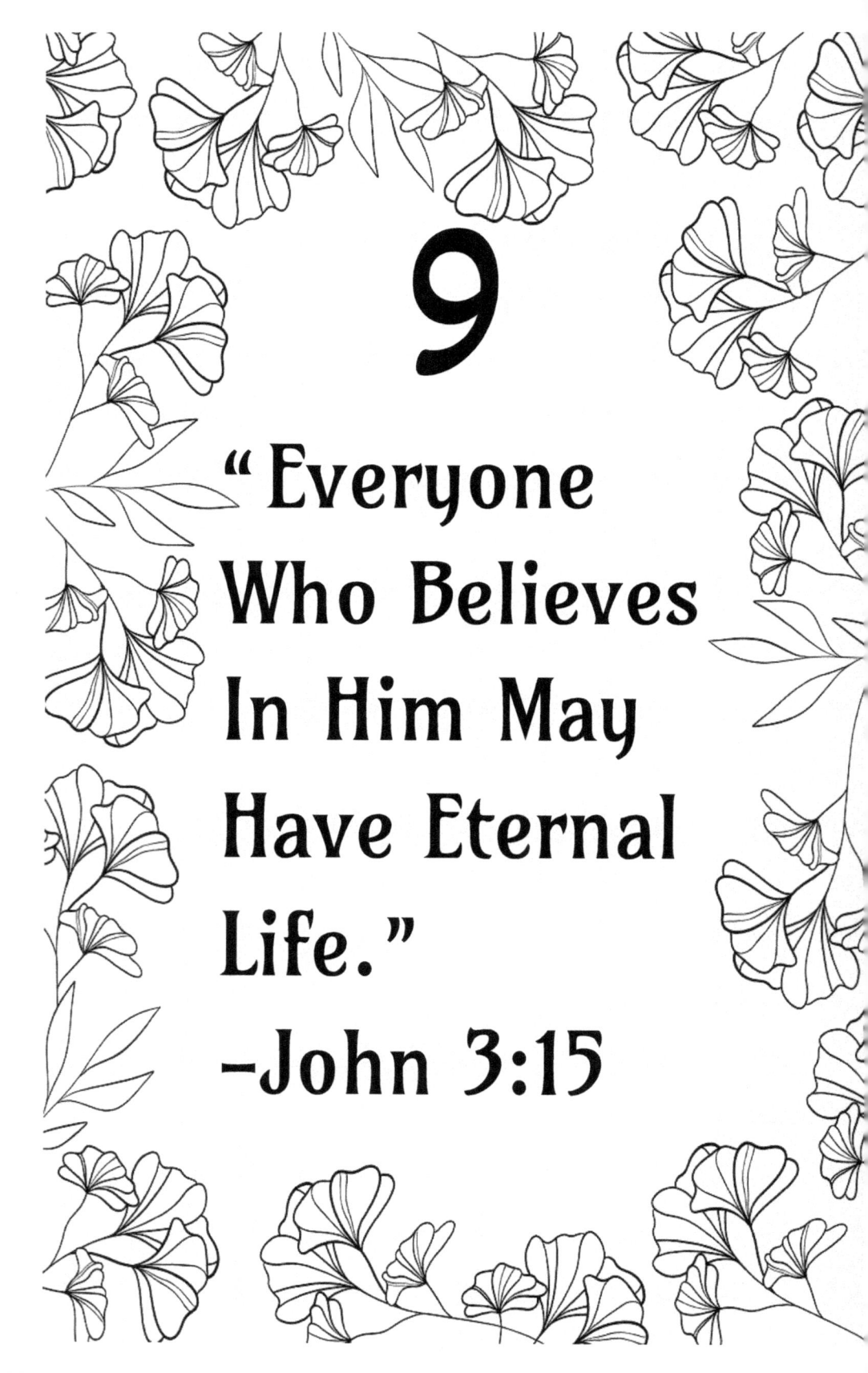

9

"Everyone Who Believes In Him May Have Eternal Life."

-John 3:15

From Death to Life

Lazarus, a close friend of Jesus, became very sick and died. Jesus arrived four days later, after Lazarus had already been buried. Martha said, "If You had been here, he wouldn't have died." But Jesus told her to trust Him. Then He went to the tomb and called out, "Lazarus, come out!" And Lazarus walked out—alive.

✝ Even when it feels too late, God is never too late. Jesus has power over death and gives us new life, hope, and healing, no matter how impossible it may seem.

Lazarus Lives

```
A L Y S L L A H V X A L V Y A L I V E N
Z A L Y N V T L J H R X B E S C I B C Q
O Z N A J S D N T H A E B U Z P W F X N
R A T L C T U R E O L N K N R S L B E X
  R X E L A A S O I Y D U H G I G H X
  U F D I M V L E V O R E R L I E K V
  S T K X N M V B J D N A Y N E P D I
  T K H O P E T D C N V W M N K B Q N
  O U           Y E           F S
  N B           P I           X B
  E W T S U R T L C R F M B H V W M L
  A S W I M I I P M F W N V N M O E L
  I E Y R E W O P C C T A Y Q T S Q S

J D N B P O W M C W O I H M S S L H V U
I T V B E W R E S U R R E C T I O N G J
K B H B E N F G A Q J E S D X U W X L V
W L Y E W N K N U P E L C A R I M P N V
O S N X M U Y F E A C G L O S U C J F H
```

LAZARUS	RESURRECTION	HOPE	DELAY
JESUS	LIFE	TRUST	GRAVE
TOMB	MARTHA	BELIEVE	CALL
STONE	MARY	FRIEND	MIRACLE
BURIED	WEEP	ALIVE	POWER

Reflection

"DID I NOT TELL YOU THAT IF YOU BELIEVE, YOU WILL SEE THE GLORY OF GOD?" – JOHN 11:40

TODAY I WILL FOLLOW GOD'S LIGHT BY...

....
....

CHOOSE A SMALL ACTION, ATTITUDE, OR WORD TO CARRY WITH YOU!

What part of your life needs Jesus to bring new life today?

....
....
....

What does this story show you about Jesus' power over life and death?

....
....
....

Lord, please bless [_____] with Your life-giving hope. Remind them that nothing is impossible for You.

NAME TWO TIMES GOD BROUGHT HOPE WHEN YOU FELT STUCK:

☐ ....

....

☐ ....

....

Today, I am Grateful for...

....
....
....

Dear Lord
About Today...

"I am the resurrection and the life."-
--John 11:25

Jesus Raised Him

"For nothing is impossible with God."
--Luke 1:37

Start here

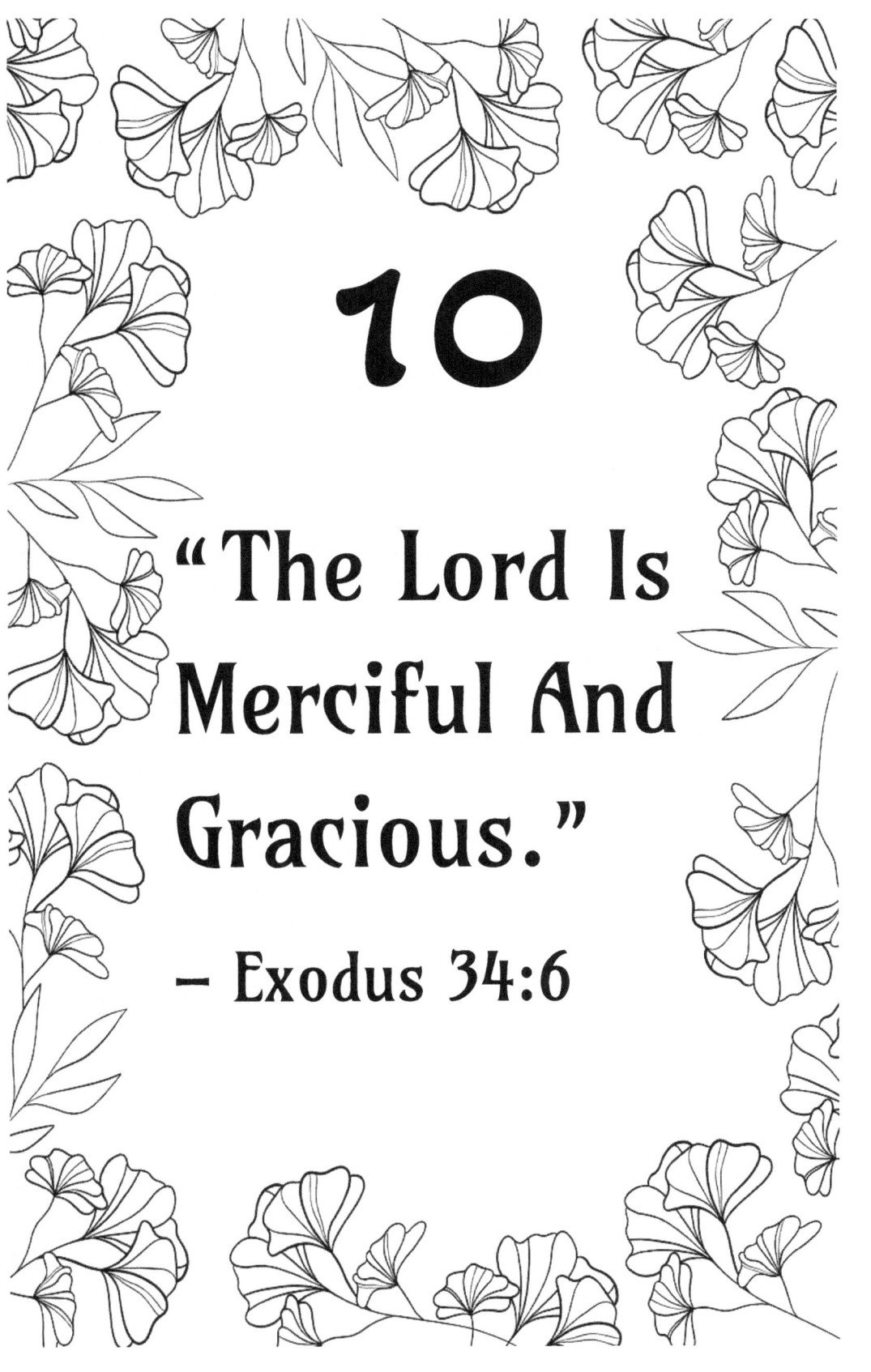

10

"The Lord Is Merciful And Gracious."

– Exodus 34:6

Found and Forgiven

Jesus told a story about a young man who asked for his inheritance and left home. He wasted it all on reckless living and ended up alone and hungry.

Ashamed, he returned home, hoping to work as a servant. But his father ran to him, wrapped him in a hug, and welcomed him with joy.

✝ No matter how far we go, God's love waits with open arms. When we return, He doesn't shame us.
He restores us.
That's the beauty of grace.

Hope & Forgiveness

R	S	3	E	F	C	Y	0	4	E	P	G	6	C	8	9
X	X	6	F	M	5	5	W	F	L	N	U	T	C	9	V
N	9	P	P	O	O	O	U	2	N	W	D	N	3	4	K
5	N	8	A	A	U	H	X	B	O	3	6	E	U	8	E
4	T	G	I	P	Y	N	O	I	S	S	A	P	M	O	C
G	6	O	5	X	O	Y	D	Z	S	C	G	E	6	E	A
0	1	S	O	J	E	P	5	8	E	V	T	R	C	H	R
A	5	V	B	9	H	Y	1	L	N	R	B	N	A	I	B
Y	A	E	M	O	C	L	E	W	E	U	A	G	E	C	M
I	3	K	P	R	1	B	H	H	V	T	E	Y	N	S	E
Y	5	E	E	9	R	N	T	U	I	X	E	V	A	T	6
9	P	M	C	A	O	A	Y	R	G	N	V	L	O	S	T
M	F	A	T	6	F	H	E	O	R	J	8	W	2	L	W
S	Z	E	J	A	I	H	9	U	O	0	O	R	J	8	3
R	E	T	U	R	N	W	O	2	F	Q	O	U	8	D	7
N	9	3	9	I	X	J	V	I	0	P	I	P	C	E	S

FATHER	LOVE	LOST	JOURNEY
SON	MERCY	FOUND	INHERITANCE
HOME	COMPASSION	RETURN	PIG
FORGIVENESS	HUG	WELCOME	HOPE
GRACE	CELEBRATE	REPENT	EMBRACE

Reflection

"THERE IS JOY IN THE PRESENCE OF THE ANGELS OF GOD OVER ONE SINNER WHO REPENTS." – LUKE 15:10

Is there someone close to you that you need to forgive—or ask forgiveness from?..................................
....
....

What does this story teach you about God's forgiveness and love?..................................
....
....

Lord, welcome [_____] back with grace. Help me love them patiently.
....

NAME TWO WAYS YOU CAN SHOW LOVE TO SOMEONE WHO MADE A MISTAKE.

☐ ....
....

☐ ....
....

Today, I am Grateful for...

....
....
....

Dear Lord, About Today...

"This son of mine was dead and is alive again; he was lost and is found." --Luke 15:24

The Father's Embrace

Start here

"There is joy in
heaven over one
sinner who repents."
--Luke 15:10

11

"This Is My Body, Given For You; Do This In Remembrance Of Me."

– Luke 22:19

The Bread of Life

At the Last Supper, Jesus took bread, gave thanks, broke it, and gave it to His disciples, saying: "This is my body, given for you; do this in remembrance of me." Then He took the cup and said: "This cup is the new covenant in my blood, which is poured out for you." That night, Jesus gave us the gift of the Eucharist—a way to stay close to Him, to remember His sacrifice, and to receive His grace.

✝ When we receive the Eucharist, Jesus is truly with us, nourishing our hearts and souls. It's more than a ritual; it's a gift of healing, unity, and the promise of eternal life.

Eternal Life

```
          S  H  H  G  Q  T     T  C
          A  S  L  O  F  U     S  O
          C  I  P  I  L  S     I  M
          T  R  R  G        Y  R  M  H
          A  I  U  T        K  A  U  T
          B  F  O           H  N  I
          L  I  N  G        R  C  I  A
          E  C  H  U        X  U  O  F
          E  I  G  R  A  C  E  N

    F     R  E  P  P  U  S  T  S  A  L     R
       R  E  M  E  M  B  R  A  N  C  E  T
       D  D  J  Q  Y  T  I  N  U  T  N  O
       G  N  I  V  I  G  S  K  N  A  H  T
          W  D  R  D  J  E  N  B
             A  E  O  E
             P  S  E  V  O  B
             K  U  U  O  R  Z  L  O
          A  S  E  C  C  F  B  Q  B  D
          D  I  S  C  I  P  L  E  S  B  V  Y
```

EUCHARIST	BREAD	DISCIPLES	TABLE
BODY	CUP	COMMUNION	FAITH
BLOOD	THANKSGIVING	GRACE	NOURISH
JESUS	SACRIFICE	GIFT	HOLY
COVENANT	LAST SUPPER	REMEMBRANCE	UNITY

Reflection

"I AM THE BREAD OF LIFE. WHOEVER COMES TO ME WILL NEVER GO HUNGRY." – JOHN 6:35

TODAY I WILL FOLLOW GOD'S LIGHT BY...

....
....

CHOOSE A SMALL ACTION, ATTITUDE, OR WORD TO CARRY WITH YOU!

Is there something heavy on your heart you want to give to Jesus?

....
....
....
....

What is one promise you want to make to Jesus today?

....
....
....
....

Lord, feed the heart of [_____] with Your love. Show me how to serve them with kindness.

....

NAME TWO SHORT PRAYERS YOU SAY TO JESUS AFTER RECEIVING THE EUCHARIST:

☐....................
....
☐....................
....

Today, I am Grateful for...

....
....
....

Dear Lord
About Today...

"I am the bread of life." -John 6:35

The Bread of Life

"Whoever eats this bread will live forever."
— John 6:51

Start here

12

"My God will meet all your needs."

Philippians 4:19 –

God Provides

A crowd of over 5,000 followed Jesus to hear Him teach. When it grew late, the disciples wanted to send them away to find food—but Jesus said, "You give them something to eat." All they had were five loaves and two fish. Jesus took the food, gave thanks, broke it, and handed it to the crowd. Everyone ate—and there were twelve baskets left over.

✝ God can do big things with small offerings. When we give what we have (our time, talents, or trust) He multiplies it. He knows your needs and is always able to provide, even when it seems impossible.

More Than Enough

```
        Y  R  G  N  U  H  P
     E  N  Z  H  D  R  R  V  D
  C  L  Z  D  D  Q  O  G  Z  E  T  N              O  W  T
P  Y  C  ★     E  V  H  N  V  L  W  F  B           K  D  V
V  S  A     C  I  I  L  I  C  P  E  H  I  A        V  I  B
F  D  R  K  D  D  U  F  S  P  T  L  F  X  S  Z     L  S  X
D  B  I  E  W  Z  Y  L  S  Q  Q  V  W  T  T  H  O  H  C  K
S  G  M  O  G  J  N  Q  E  I  A  E  E  Q  O  A  L  T  I  W
S  K  R  F  A  I  T  H  L  O  T  K  Q  N  V  V  C  S  P  I
R  C  N  H  C  D  R  C  B  T  S  A  G  E  T  S  E  F  L  C
E  C  N  A  D  N  U  B  A  A  A  B  S  M  W  T  H  R  E  M
   A  P  H  H  M  I  P  B  J  E  S  U  S  S        A  S  J
      N  J  B  T  N  R  G  D  M  T  L  I           O  R  U
         C  M  U  L  T  I  P  L  Y                 I  I  E
```

JESUS	TWO	ABUNDANCE	DISCIPLES
LOAVES	TWELVE	FAITH	HUNGRY
FISH	BASKETS	SATISFIED	LEFTOVERS
CROWD	THANKS	MIRACLE	BLESSING
FIVE	PROVIDE	MULTIPLY	SHARE

Reflection

"MY GOD WILL SUPPLY ALL YOUR NEEDS." –
PHILIPPIANS 4:19

TODAY I WILL FOLLOW GOD'S LIGHT BY...

....

....

CHOOSE A SMALL ACTION, ATTITUDE, OR WORD TO CARRY WITH YOU!

When has God provided for you in an unexpected way?

....

....

....

What does this story teach you about trusting God with what you have?

....

....

....

....

Lord, provide for [_____] today. Use me to bring joy and peace to them.

....

NAME TWO SMALL GIFT OR TALENT THAT YOU WILL OFFER TO GOD THIS WEEK:

☐ ....

....

☐ ....

....

Today, I am Grateful for...

....

....

....

Dear Lord, About Today...

"Jesus then took the loaves, gave thanks, and distributed to those who were seated as much as they wanted."--John 6:11

More Than Enough

Start here

"From his fullness we have all received, grace upon grace."
— John 1:16

13

"The Lord Is My Light And My Salvation— Whom Shall I Fear?"
-Psalm 27:1

Sent to Shine

After Jesus rose from the dead, He appeared to His disciples and gave them a mission: :As the Father sent Me, now I am sending you." He breathed on them and said, "Receive the Holy Spirit."

This wasn't just a goodbye—it was a beginning. Jesus was saying, "Now it's your turn. Go be My light in the world."

✝ You are sent with purpose.
Jesus has called you to bring light, love, and truth to the places you live, learn, and work.
Even small acts of kindness or courage can reflect God's light.

Light of the World

```
U V H Y O T R Y E D U T I T A R G H Z M
T O E B I F K E V M N Q F J G U Z O B G
K B T R   F Q                 H A I T
O N I G   D N A M M O C H B Q T   K T
X P B X   G L                 I   D C
S Q D J   A W           Z     A   P F
Z Y J Z   I B           K     F   I A
W T U D   N H       G Z O     B   S Y
Q I Q I   M O           P     D   U T
J N N S   S P           O     H B A H
E R Y C   Y E           D     M E D T
B E X I   K S                 W V I Z
G T K P   B I                 W   P E
E E N L   J F O L L O W Q R M S   R J
A Z O E   Q E H           H H     O O
T V I S   Y   S L H W T H A F   L M K
E S S T U     I U T K O R C     Z I G
T T S B P A G G A F S I E R U A G B S G
D F I Y O A H E B L E S S E D T E P E W
H U M Q B T B A D O Z P F B T L H T R X
```

BLESSED TEACH OBEY WORD
SHARE BAPTIZE TRUTH FAITH
JESUS COMMAND LOVE MISSION
GRATITUDE PROMISE FOLLOW HOPE
DISCIPLES SPIRIT ETERNITY LIGHT

Light of the World

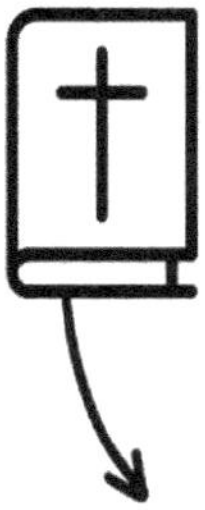

Start here

the *bible* is our compass

Reflection

"AS THE FATHER HAS SENT ME, I AM SENDING YOU." –
JOHN 20:21

TODAY I WILL FOLLOW GOD'S LIGHT BY...

....

....

CHOOSE A SMALL ACTION, ATTITUDE, OR WORD TO CARRY WITH YOU!

What's one truth from this book you want to keep living out every day?

....

....

....

Where has God placed you to be a light right now? (school, work, home, friends)

....

....

....

Lord, help me share Your love with [_____].
Please let them hear your Truth and Encouragement.

NAME TWO WAYS YOU CAN SHARE GOD'S LOVE IN YOUR DAILY LIFE

☐ ....

....

☐ ....

....

Today, I am Grateful for...

....

....

....

Dear Lord
About Today...

"Let your light shine before others." – Matthew 5:16

I Love Jesus

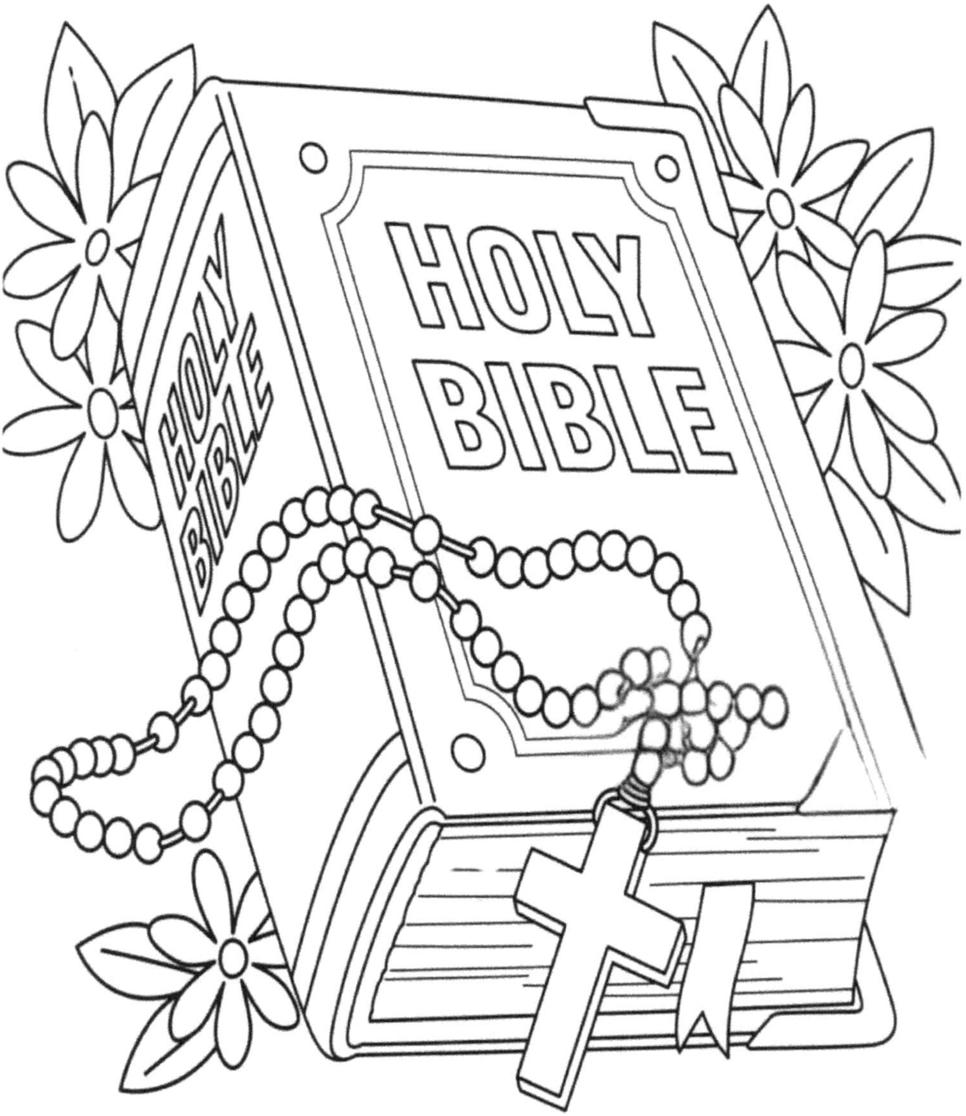

Closing Prayer
✝

Lord, thank You for walking with me through every page. May the truths I've discovered take root in my heart. Help me live with purpose, love others deeply, and trust You more each day.

Wherever I go from here, remind me I'm never alone. Amen.

✝ Reflect. Share. Inspire.

JMJ Journal is blessed to have
joined you on your spiritual path.

If this journal has encouraged or
uplifted you in any way,
would you kindly consider leaving a
short review on Amazon?

Your words can help others find
hope, reflection, and joy through
this journal too.

We'd Love Your Feedback!

https://www.amazon.com/reiview/create-review?&asin=B0F6K8PLCK

Solutions

The Lord's Prayer
Solution #1

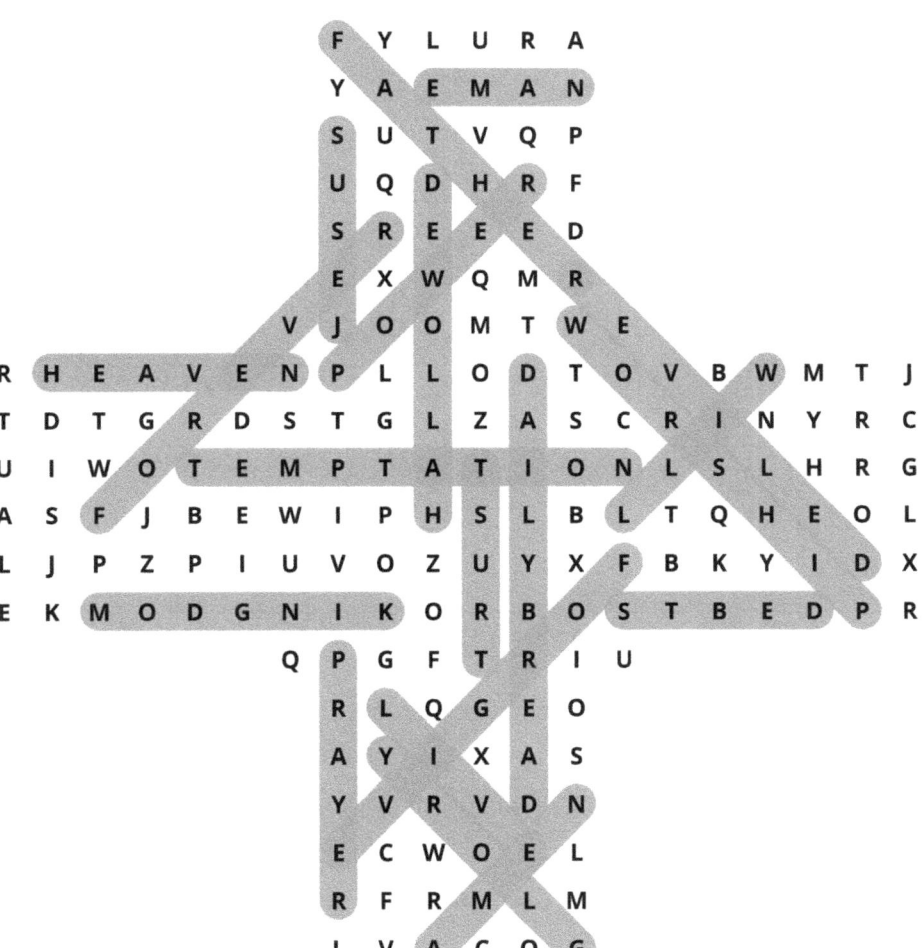

PRAYER	NAME	DEBTS	POWER
JESUS	KINGDOM	TEMPTATION	FOREVER
FATHER	WILL	DELIVER	AMEN
HEAVEN	DAILY BREAD	EVIL	TRUST
HALLOWED	FORGIVE	GLORY	WORSHIP

Come Holy Spirit: Solution

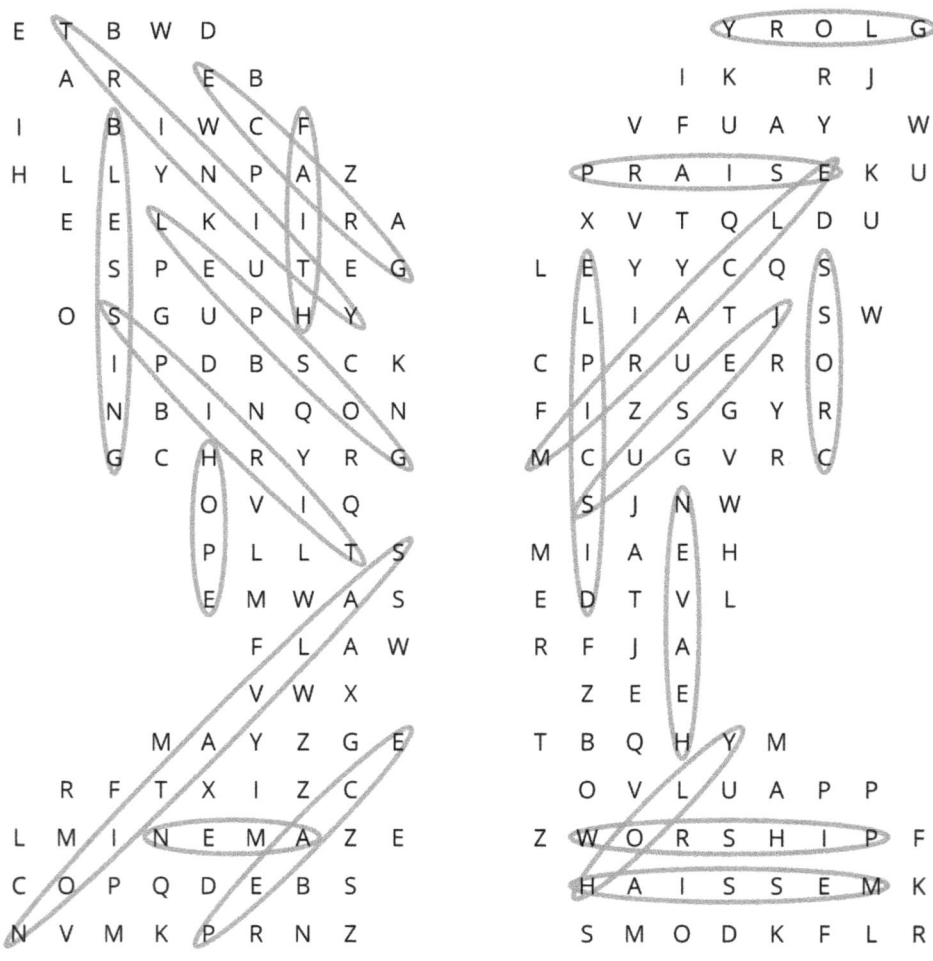

FAITH   PRAISE   PEACE   GLORY

GRACE   HEAVEN   HOPE   DISCIPLE

JESUS   SALVATION   MESSIAH   WORSHIP

HOLY   BLESSING   SPIRIT   AMEN

GOSPEL   MIRACLE   TRINITY   CROSS

Peace, Be Still
Solution

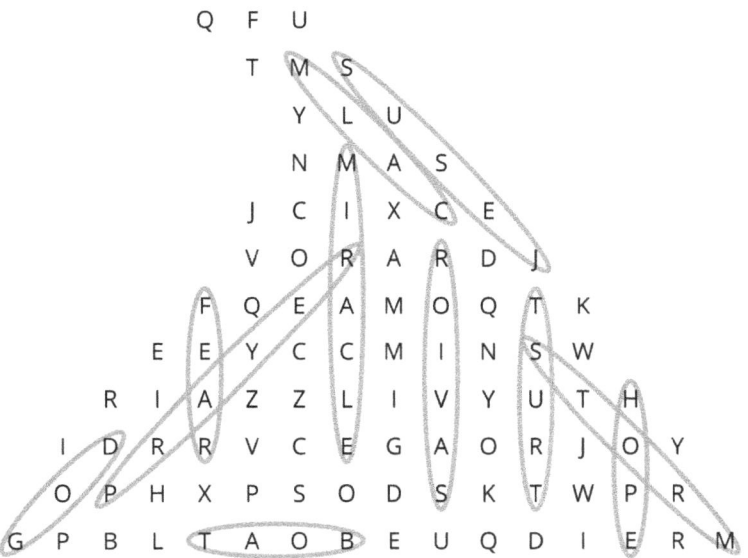

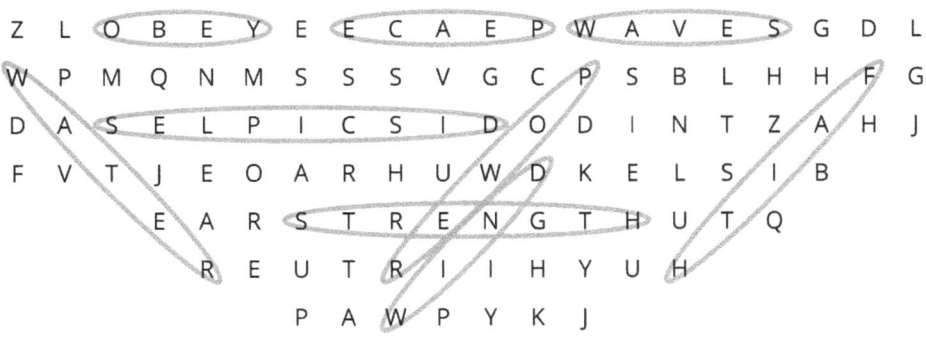

STORM	WAVES	BOAT	POWER
FAITH	WIND	MIRACLE	HOPE
JESUS	FEAR	WATER	GOD
PEACE	CALM	OBEY	SAVIOR
DISCIPLES	TRUST	PRAYER	STRENGTH

Love in Action: Solution

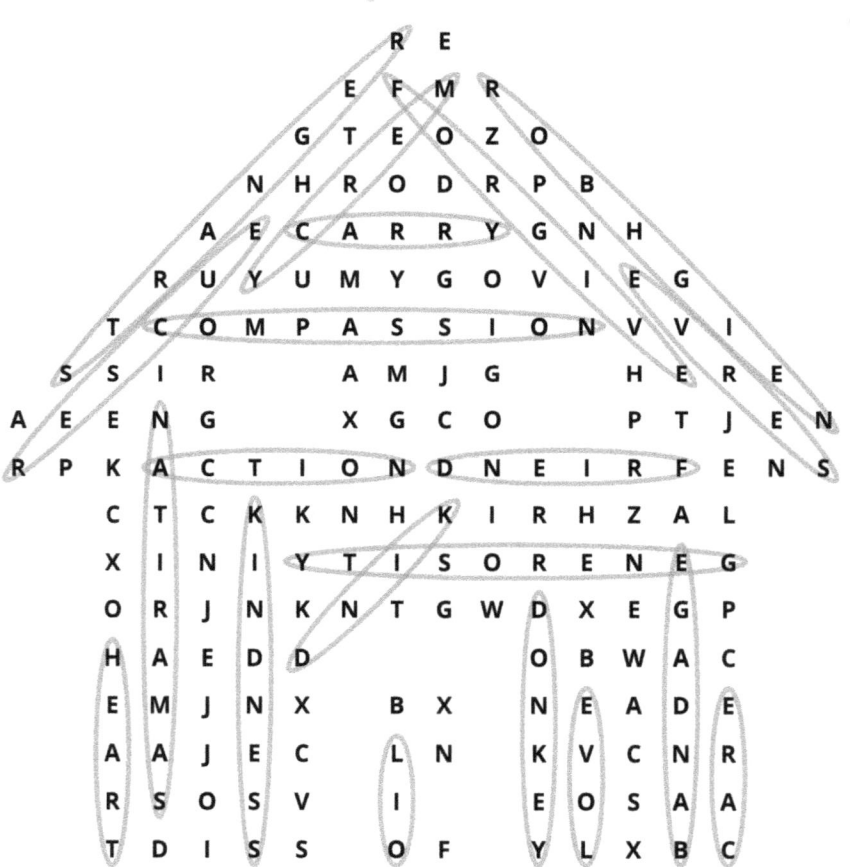

FORGIVE	NEIGHBOR	CARE	DONKEY
KIND	LOVE	RESCUE	OIL
ACTION	KINDNESS	STRANGER	BANDAGE
FRIEND	MERCY	HEART	GENEROSITY
SERVE	SAMARITAN	CARRY	COMPASSION

Now I See
Solution

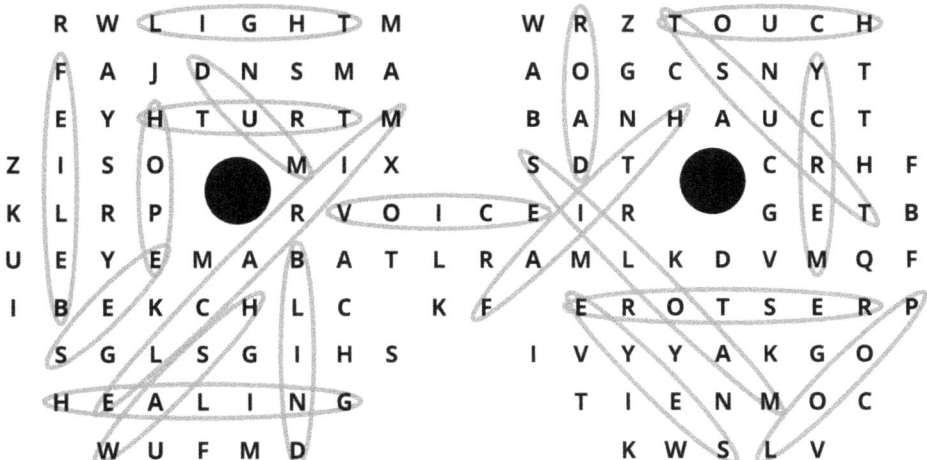

R	W	L	I	G	H	T	M		W	R	Z	T	O	U	C	H
F	A	J	D	N	S	M	A		A	O	G	C	S	N	Y	T
E	Y	H	T	U	R	T	M		B	A	N	H	A	U	C	T
Z	I	S	O		M	I	X		S	D	T		C	R	H	F
K	L	R	P	R	V	O	I	C	E	I	R		G	E	T	B
U	E	Y	E	M	A	B	A	T	L	R	A	M	L	K	D	V	M	Q	F
I	B	E	K	C	H	L	C		K	F	E	R	O	T	S	E	R	P
	S	G	L	S	G	I	H	S		I	V	Y	Y	A	K	G	O
	H	E	A	L	I	N	G			T	I	E	N	M	O	C
	W	U	F	M	D					K	W	S	L	V

BLIND	**SEE**	**MIRACLE**	**RESTORE**
HEALING	**WASH**	**BELIEF**	**VOICE**
MUD	**POOL**	**TRUST**	**TOUCH**
EYES	**SILOAM**	**LIGHT**	**MERCY**
FAITH	**ROAD**	**TRUTH**	**HOPE**

Guided By The Light Solutioin

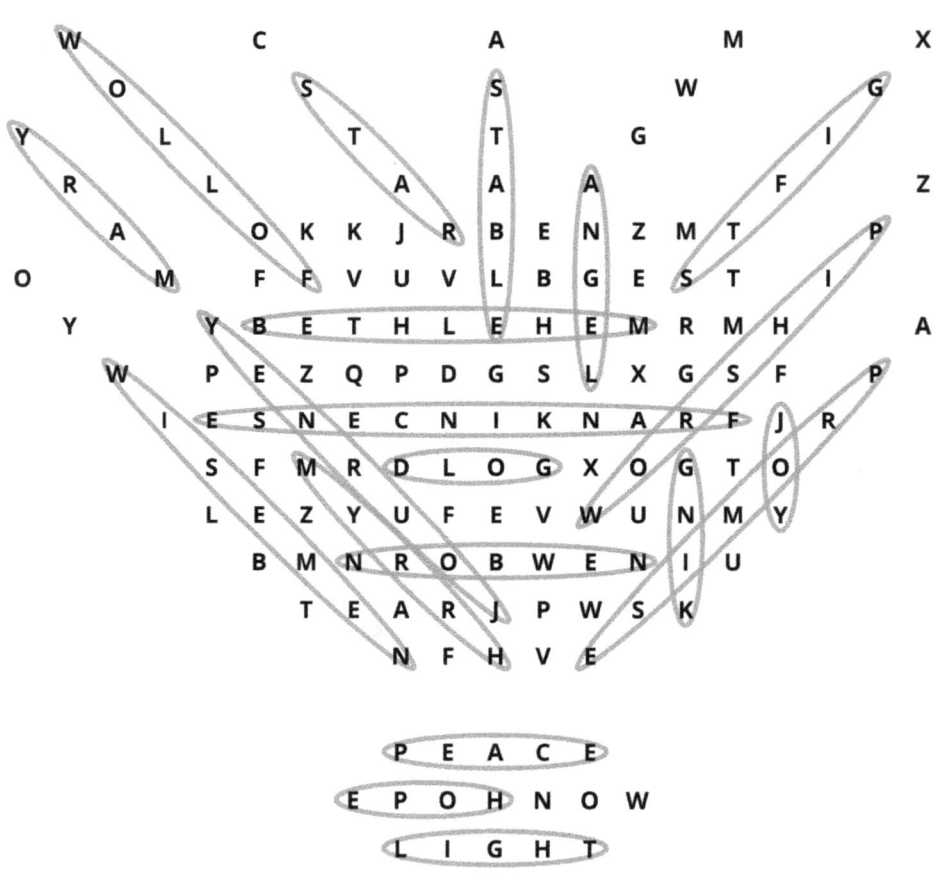

STAR	GIFTS	WORSHIP	JOY
LIGHT	GOLD	MARY	ANGEL
WISE MEN	FRANKINCENSE	STABLE	PROMISE
BETHLEHEM	MYRRH	NEWBORN	FOLLOW
KING	JOURNEY	PEACE	HOPE

A Grateful Heart
Solution

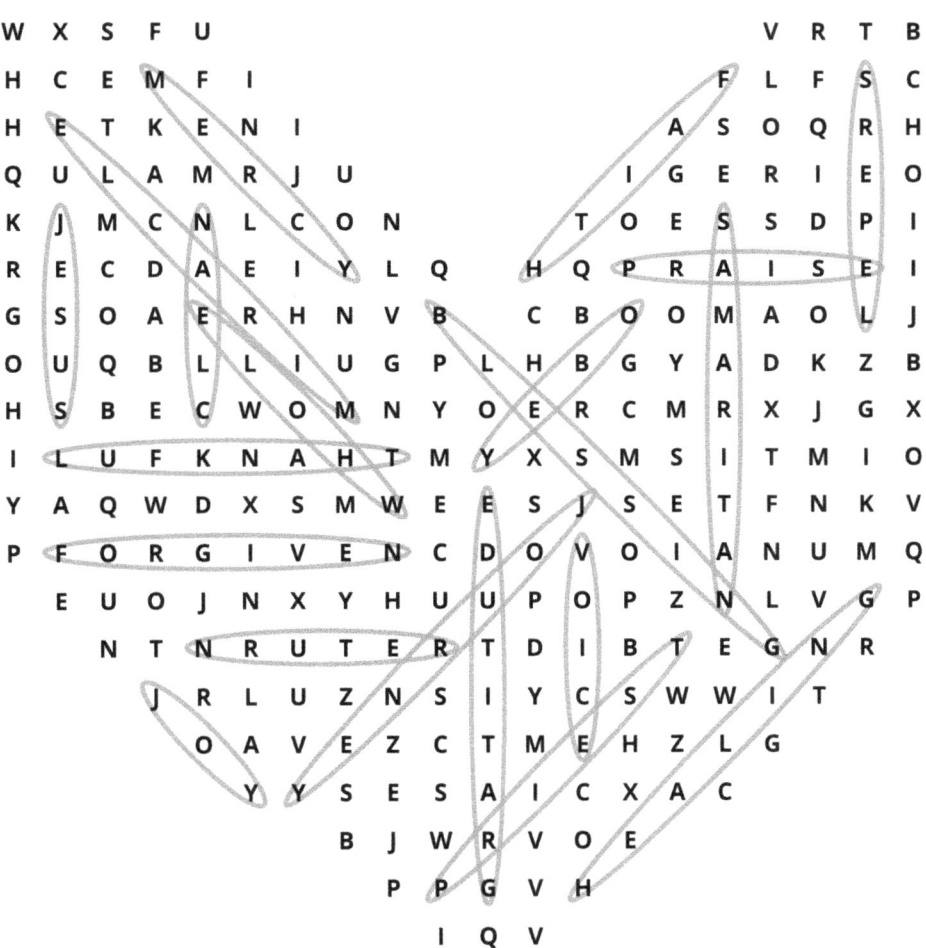

W X S F U   V R T B
H C E M F I   F L F S C
H E T K E N I   A S O Q R H
Q U L A M R J U   I G E R I E O
K J M C N L C O N   T O E S S D P I
R E C D A E I Y L Q   H Q P R A I S E I
G S O A E R H N V B   C B O O M A O L J
O U Q B L L I U G P L H B G Y A D K Z B
H S B E C W O M N Y O E R C M R X J G X
I L U F K N A H T M Y X S M S I T M I O
Y A Q W D X S M W E E S J S E T F N K V
P F O R G I V E N C D O V O I A N U M Q
E U O J N X Y H U U P O P Z N L V G P
N T N R U T E R T D I B T E G N R
J R L U Z N S I Y C S W W I T
O A V E Z C T M E H Z L G
Y Y S E S A I C X A C
B J W R V O E
P P G V H
I Q V

LEPERS	THANKFUL	PRAISE	RETURN
GRATITUDE	SAMARITAN	CLEAN	OBEY
FAITH	PRIEST	BLESSING	FORGIVEN
MERCY	JESUS	MIRACLE	JOURNEY
HEALING	WHOLE	VOICE	JOY

A Widow's Gift
Solution

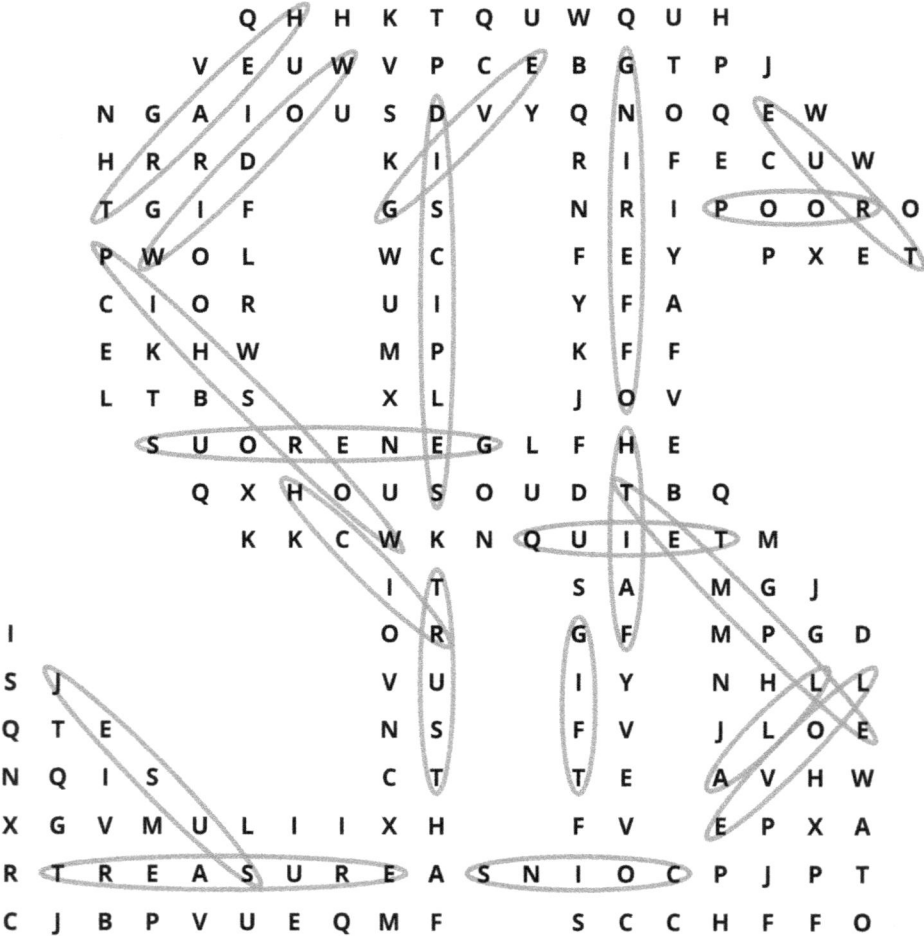

WIDOW	**TEMPLE**	**TREASURE**	**DISCIPLES**
OFFERING	**COINS**	**JESUS**	**GIFT**
HEART	**RICH**	**POOR**	**QUIET**
GIVE	**TRUST**	**ALL**	**GENEROUS**
FAITH	**LOVE**	**WORSHIP**	**TRUE**

Lazarus Lives
Solution

```
A L Y S L L A H V X A L V Y A L I V E N
Z A L Y N V T L J H R X B E S C I B C Q
O Z N A J S D N T H A E B U Z P W F X N
R A T L C T U R E O L N K N R S L B E X
R X E L A A S O I Y D U H G I G H X
U F D I M V L E V O R E R L I E K V
S T K X N M V B J D N A Y N E P D I
T K H O P E T D C N V W M N K B Q N
O U Y E F S
N B P I X B
E W T S U R T L C R F M B H V W M L
A S W I M I I P M F W N V N M O E L
I E Y R E W O P C C T A Y Q T S Q S

J D N B P O W M C W O I H M S S L H V U
I T V B E W R E S U R R E C T I O N G J
K B H B E N F G A Q J E S D X U W X L V
W L Y E W N K N U P E L C A R I M P N V
O S N X M U Y F E A C G L O S U C J F H
```

LAZARUS	RESURRECTION	HOPE	DELAY
JESUS	LIFE	TRUST	GRAVE
TOMB	MARTHA	BELIEVE	CALL
STONE	MARY	FRIEND	MIRACLE
BURIED	WEEP	ALIVE	POWER

Hope & Forgiveness
Solution

R	S	3	E	F	C	Y	0	4	E	P	G	6	C	8	9
X	X	6	F	M	5	5	W	F	L	N	U	T	C	9	V
N	9	P	P	O	O	O	U	2	N	W	D	N	3	4	K
5	N	8	A	A	U	H	X	B	O	3	6	E	U	8	E
4	T	G	I	P	Y	N	O	I	S	S	A	P	M	O	C
G	6	O	5	X	O	Y	D	Z	S	C	G	E	6	E	A
0	1	S	O	J	E	P	5	8	E	V	T	R	C	H	R
A	5	V	B	9	H	Y	1	L	N	R	B	N	A	I	B
Y	A	E	M	O	C	L	E	W	E	U	A	G	E	C	M
I	3	K	P	R	1	B	H	H	V	T	E	Y	N	S	E
Y	5	E	E	9	R	N	T	U	I	X	E	V	A	T	6
9	P	M	C	A	O	A	Y	R	G	N	V	L	O	S	T
M	F	A	T	6	F	H	E	0	R	J	8	W	2	L	W
S	Z	E	J	A	I	H	9	U	O	0	O	R	J	8	3
R	E	T	U	R	N	W	O	2	F	Q	O	U	8	D	7
N	9	3	9	I	X	J	V	I	0	P	I	P	C	E	S

FATHER	LOVE	LOST	JOURNEY
SON	MERCY	FOUND	INHERITANCE
HOME	COMPASSION	RETURN	PIG
FORGIVENESS	HUG	WELCOME	HOPE
GRACE	CELEBRATE	REPENT	EMBRACE

Eternal Life Solution

More Than Enough
Solution

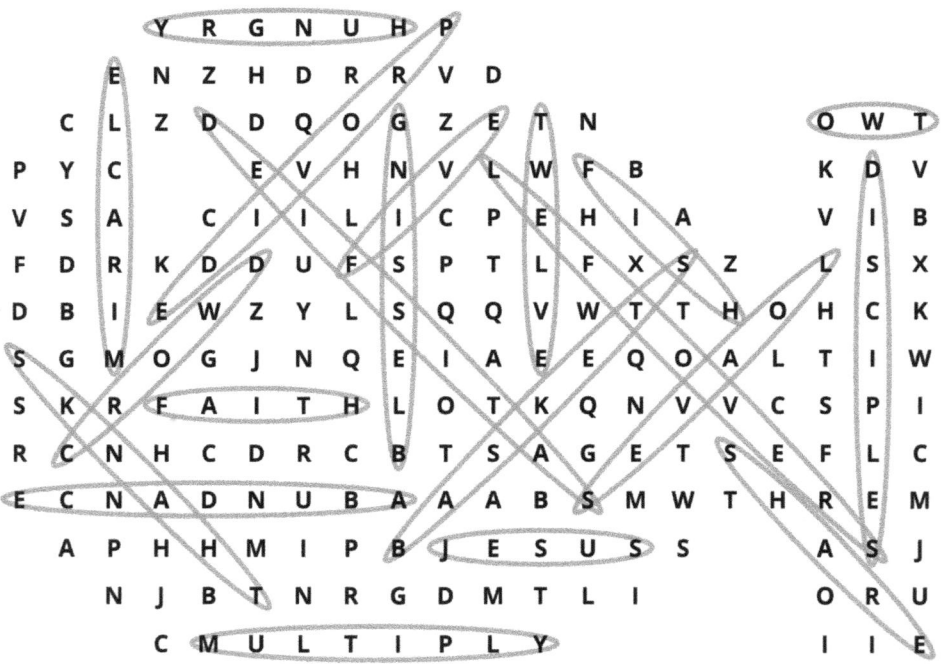

Y R G N U H P
E N Z H D R R V D
C L Z D D Q O G Z E T N   O W T
P Y C E V H N V L W F B   K D V
V S A C I I L I C P E H I A   V I B
F D R K D D U F S P T L F X S Z L S X
D B I E W Z Y L S Q Q V W T T H O H C K
S G M O G J N Q E I A E E Q O A L T I W
S K R F A I T H L O T K Q N V V C S P I
R C N H C D R C B T S A G E T S E F L C
E C N A D N U B A A A B S M W T H R E M
A P H H M I P B J E S U S S   A S J
N J B T N R G D M T L I   O R U
C M U L T I P L Y   I I E

JESUS   TWO   ABUNDANCE   DISCIPLES
LOAVES   TWELVE   FAITH   HUNGRY
FISH   BASKETS   SATISFIED   LEFTOVERS
CROWD   THANKS   MIRACLE   BLESSING
FIVE   PROVIDE   MULTIPLY   SHARE

Light of the World
Solution

```
U  V  H  Y  O  T  R  Y  E  D  U  T  I  T  A  R  G  H  Z  M
T  O  E  B  I  F  K  E  V  M  N  Q  F  J  G  U  Z  O  B  G
K  B  T  R     F  Q                          H  A  I  T
O  N  I  G     D  N  A  M  M  O  C  H  B  Q  T     K  T
X  P  B  X     G  L                          I     D  C
S  Q  D  J     A  W              Z           A     P  F
Z  Y  J  Z     I  B              K           F     I  A
W  T  U  D     N  H        G  Z  O           B     S  Y
Q  I  Q  I     M  O              P           D     U  T
J  N  N  S     S  P              O           H  B  A  H
E  R  Y  C     Y  E              D           M  E  D  T
B  E  X  I     K  S                          W  V  I  Z
G  T  K  P     B  I                          W     P  E
E  E  N  L     J  F  O  L  L  O  W  Q  R  M  S     R  J
A  Z  O  E     Q  E  H                 H  H        O  O
T  V  I  S     Y     S  L  H  W  T  H  A  F     L  M  K
E  S  S  T  U        I  U  T  K  O  R  C        Z  I  G
T  T  S  B  P  A  G  G  A  F  S  I  E  R  U  A  G  B  S  G
D  F  I  Y  O  A  H  E  B  L  E  S  S  E  D  T  E  P  E  W
H  U  M  Q  B  T  B  A  D  O  Z  P  F  B  T  L  H  T  R  X
```

BLESSED	TEACH	OBEY	WORD
SHARE	BAPTIZE	TRUTH	FAITH
JESUS	COMMAND	LOVE	MISSION
GRATITUDE	PROMISE	FOLLOW	HOPE
DISCIPLES	SPIRIT	ETERNITY	LIGHT

Our Father's Maze Adventure Solution

Start here

"Lead me, Lord, in Your path of truth."
— Psalm 25:5

Led by the Spirit Solution

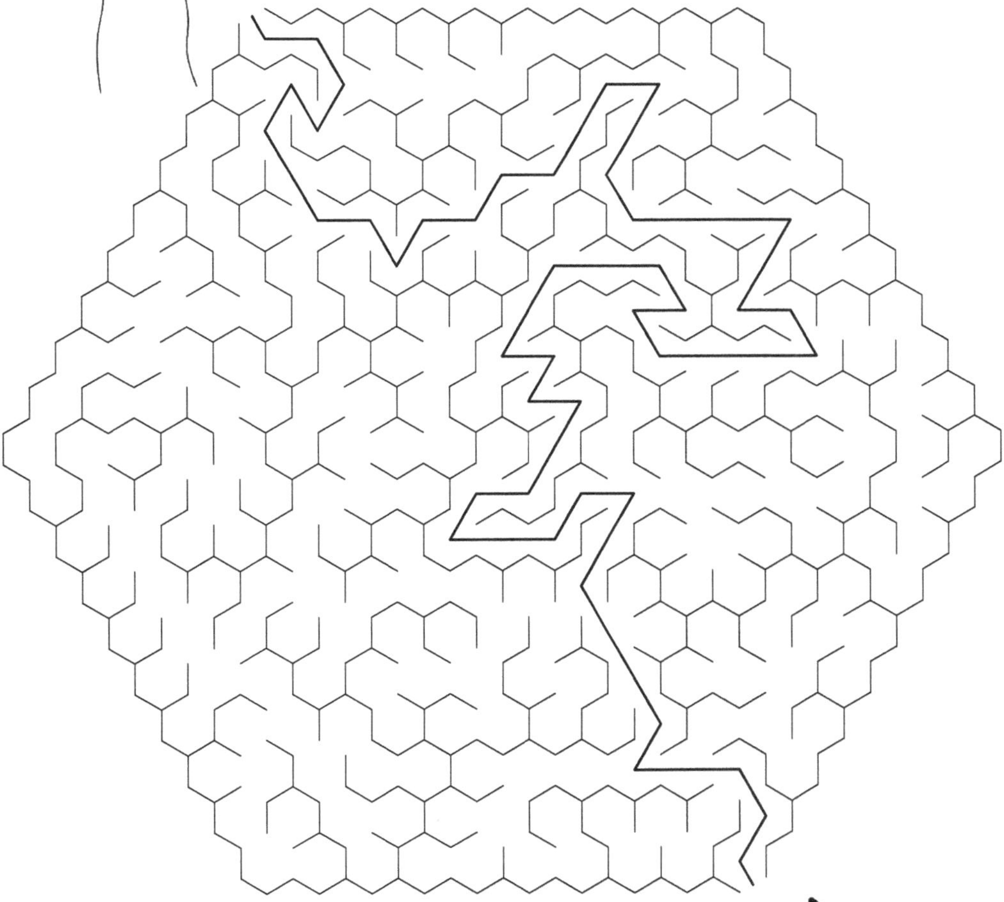

"Since we live by the
Spirit, let us keep in step
with the Spirit."
— Galatians 5:25

Start here

Peace, Be Still Solution

Start here

"Cast all your anxiety on him because he cares for you."
— 1 Peter 5:7

A Good Neighbor: Solution

"Do to others as you would have them do to you."
— Luke 6:31

Start here

"Thanks, God!" Solution

Start here

"I will give thanks to you, Lord, with all my heart." — Psalm 9:1

From Blind to Blessed: Solution

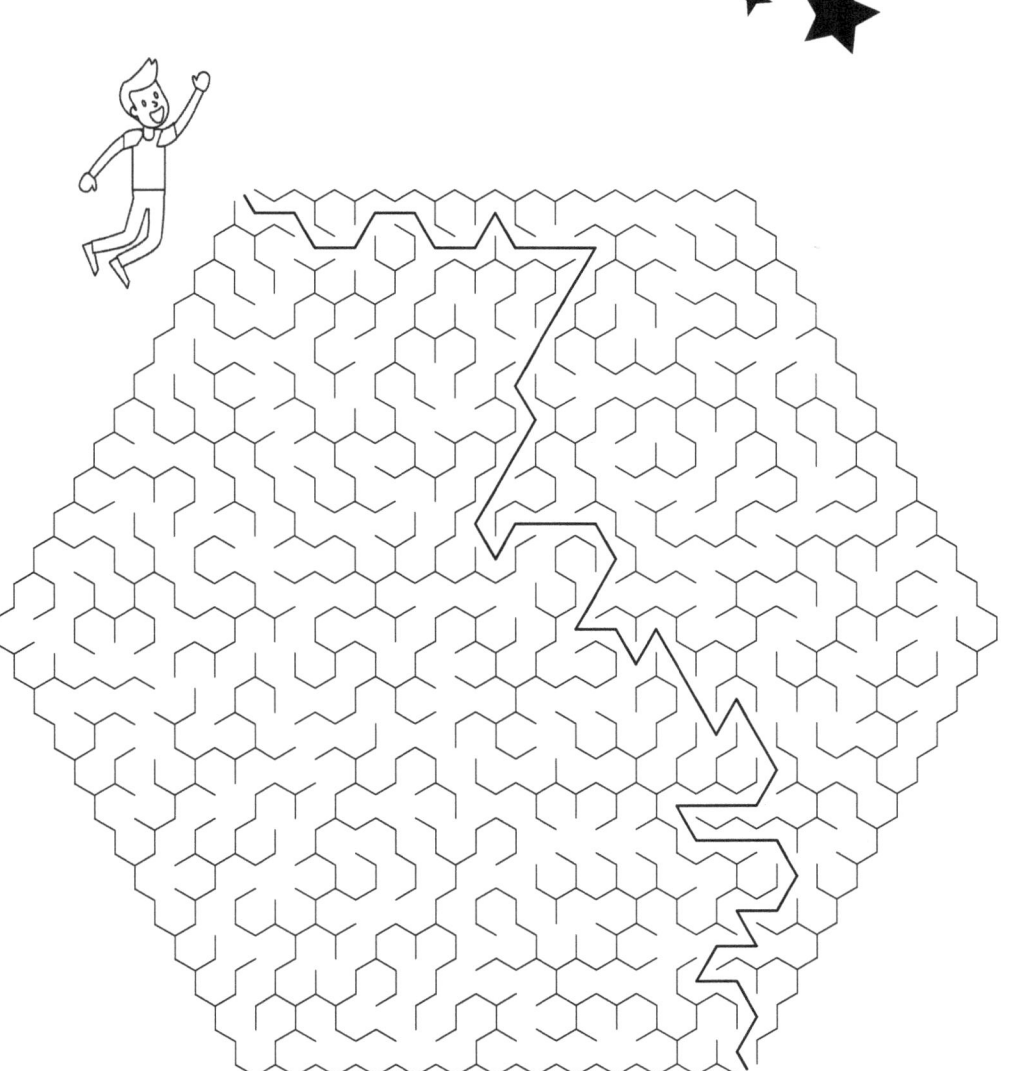

"Jesus said, 'Receive your sight; your faith has healed you.'"
— Luke 18:42

Start here

The Bread of Life Solution

"Whoever eats this bread will live forever."
— John 6:51

Start here

Follow The Star: Solution

"We saw his star when it
rose and have come to
worship him."
— Matthew 2:2

Start here

"The Widow's Gift" Solution

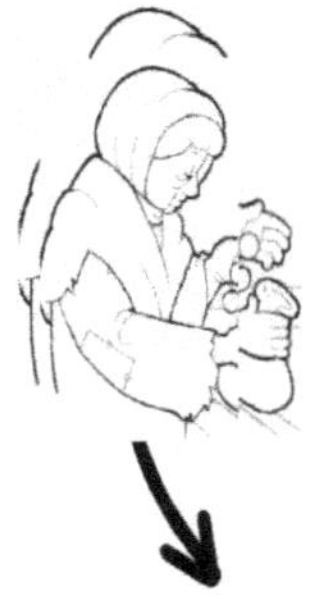

Start here

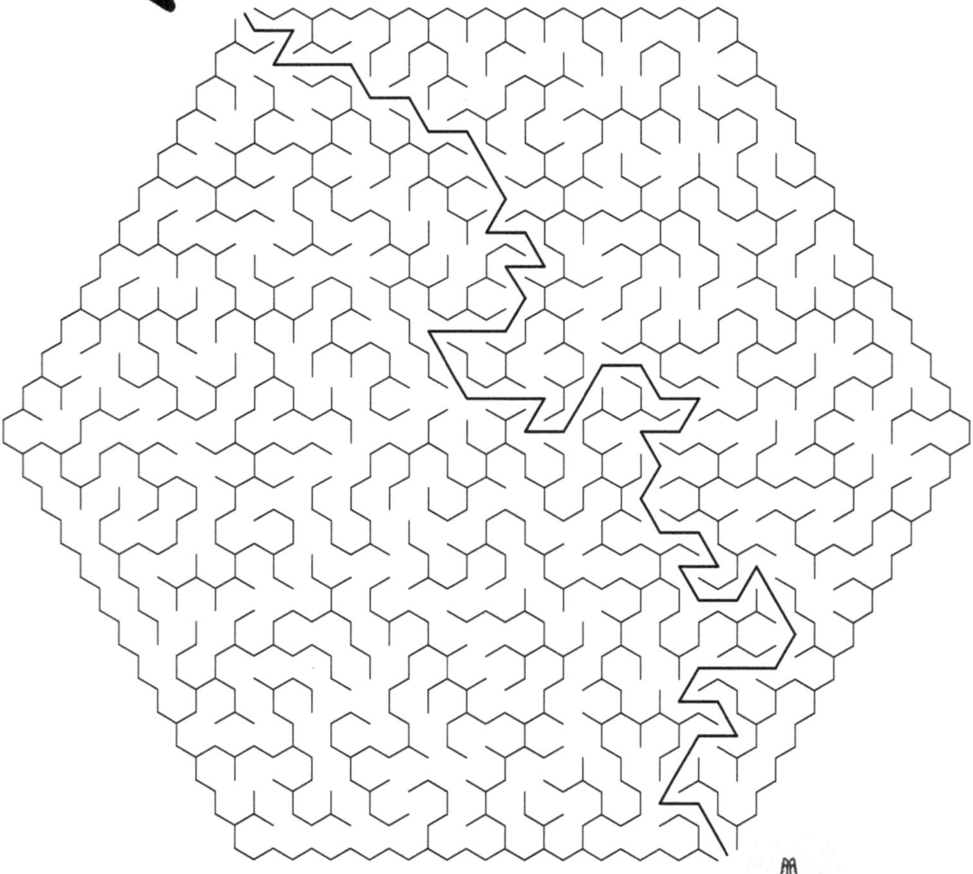

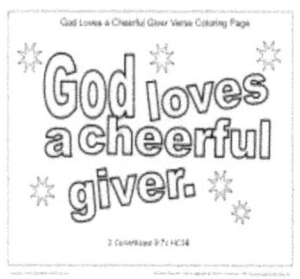

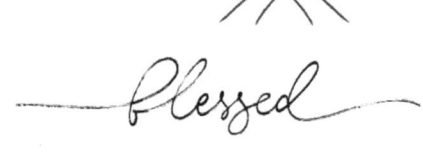

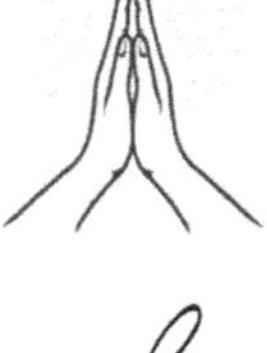

Blessed

Jesus Raised Him
Solution

Start here

The Father's Embrace
Solution

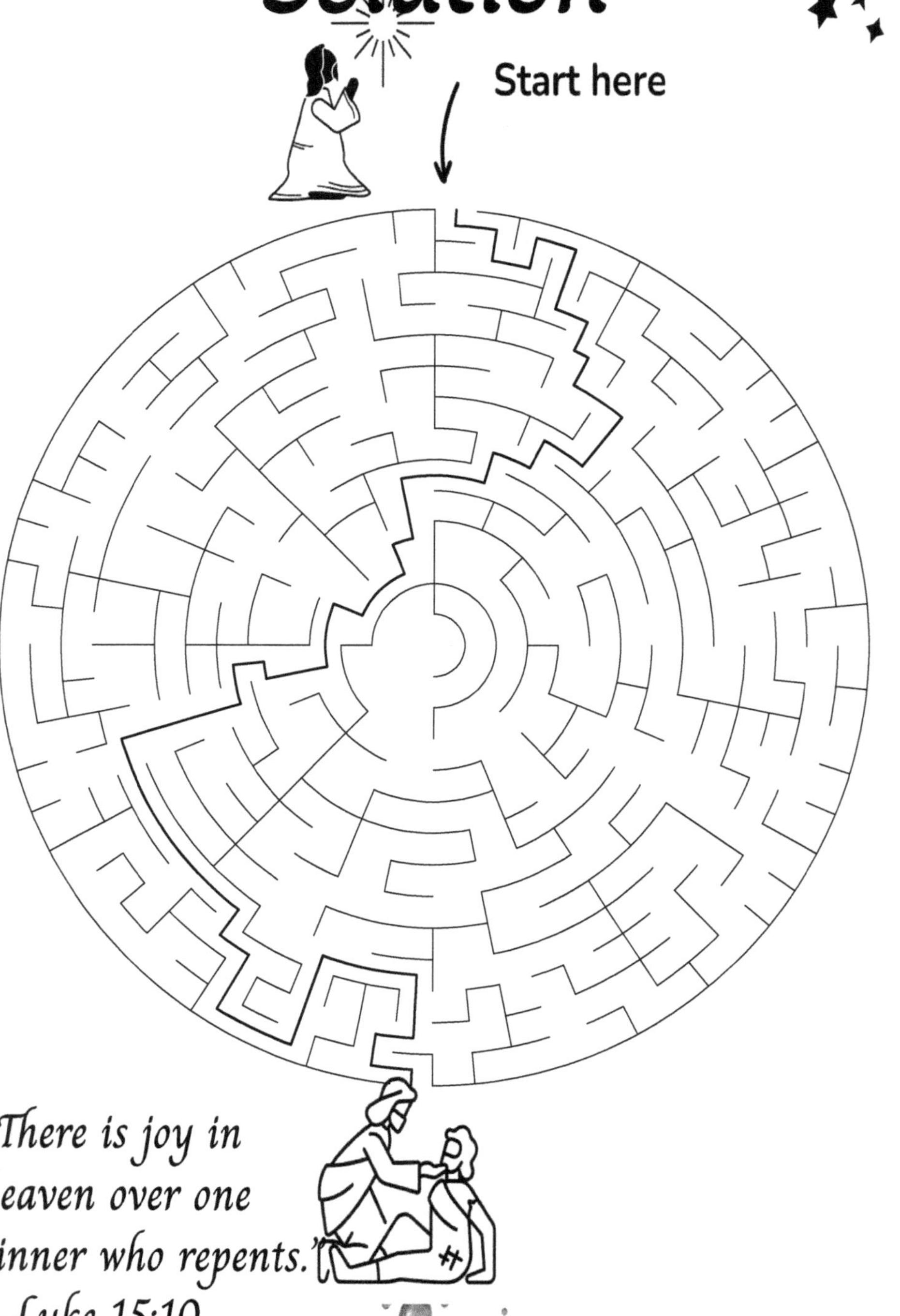

Start here

"*There is joy in heaven over one sinner who repents.*"
--Luke 15:10

More Than Enough
-Solution-

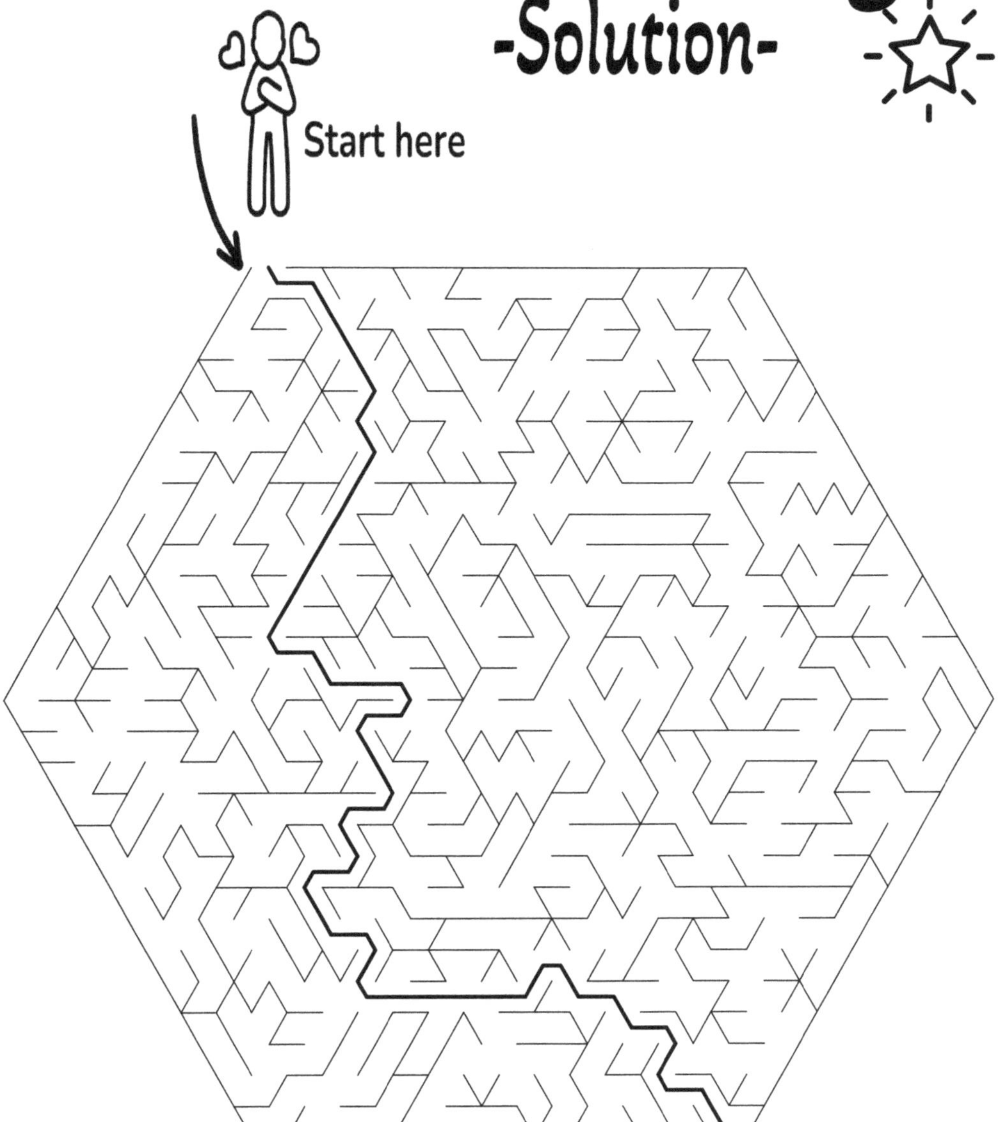

Start here

"From his fullness we have all received, grace upon grace."
— John 1:16

Light of the World
Solution

Start here

the
bible
is our
compass

www.ingramcontent.com/pod-product-compliance
Lightning Source LLC
Chambersburg PA
CBHW051534120626
46551CB00012B/1213